Murder

by Diane Yancey

LUCENT BOOKS

An imprint of Thomson Gale, a part of The Thomson Corporation

THOMSON

—✦— ™

GALE

Detroit • New York • San Francisco • San Diego • New Haven, Conn. • Waterville, Maine • London • Munich

Acknowledgement

We would like to express our sincere gratitude to FBI Special Agent Barry Vecchioni and San Diego Police Department Crime Lab Manager Michael Grubb for their invaluable reviews of Lucent's *Crime Scene Investigations: Murder.*

© 2006 Thomson Gale, a part of The Thomson Corporation.

Thomson and Star Logo are trademarks and Gale and Lucent Books are registered trademarks used herein under license.

For more information, contact
Lucent Books
27500 Drake Rd.
Farmington Hills, MI 48331-3535
Or you can visit our Internet site at http://www.gale.com

LIBRARY OF CONGRESS CATALOGING-IN-PUBLICATION DATA

Yancey, Diane.
    Murder: crime scene investigations / By Diane Yancey.
        p. cm. — (Crime Scene Investigations)
    Includes bibliographical references and index.
    ISBN 1-59018-619-2 (hard cover : alk. paper)
    1. Criminal investigation—Juvenile literature. 2. Murder—Investigation—Juvenile literature. 3. Evidence, Criminal—Juvenile literature. 4. Forensic sciences—Juvenile literature. I. Title. II. Series.
    HV8073.8.Y36 2005
    363.25'9523—dc22
                                                                    2005003112

Printed in the United States of America

Contents

Foreword

The popularity of crime scene and investigative crime shows on television has come as a surprise to many who work in the field. The main surprise is the concept that crime scene analysts are the true crime solvers, when in truth, it takes dozens of people, doing many different jobs, to solve a crime. Often, the crime scene analyst's contribution is a small one. One Minnesota forensic scientist says that the public "has gotten the wrong idea. Because I work in a lab similar to the ones on CSI, people seem to think I'm solving crimes left and right—just me and my microscope. They don't believe me when I tell them that it's the investigators that are solving crimes, not me."

Crime scene analysts do have an important role to play, however. Science has rapidly added a whole new dimension to gathering and assessing evidence. Modern crime labs can match a hair of a murder suspect to one found on a murder victim, for example, or recover a latent fingerprint from a threatening letter, or use a powerful microscope to match tool marks made during the wiring of an explosive device to a tool in a suspect's possession.

Probably the most exciting of the forensic scientist's tools is DNA analysis. DNA can be found in just one drop of blood, a dribble of saliva on a toothbrush, or even the residue from a fingerprint. Some DNA analysis techniques enable scientists to tell with certainty, for example, whether a drop of blood on a suspect's shirt is that of a murder victim.

While these exciting techniques are now an essential part of many investigations, they cannot solve crimes alone. "DNA doesn't come with a name and address on it," says the Minnesota forensic scientist. "It's great if you have someone in custody to match the sample to, but otherwise, it doesn't help.

That's the investigator's job. We can have all the great DNA evidence in the world, and without a suspect, it will just sit on the shelf. We've all seen cases with very little forensic evidence get solved by the resourcefulness of a detective."

While forensic specialists get the most media attention today, the work of detectives still forms the core of most criminal investigations. Their job, in many ways, has changed little over the years. Most cases are still solved through the persistence and determination of a criminal detective whose work may be anything but glamorous. Many cases require routine, even mind-numbing tasks. After the July 2005 bombings in London, for example, police officers sat in front of video players watching thousands of hours of closed-circuit television tape from security cameras throughout the city, and as a result were able to get the first images of the bombers.

The Lucent Books Crime Scene Investigations series explores the variety of ways crimes are solved. Titles cover particular crimes such as murder, specific cases such as the killing of three civil rights workers in Mississippi, or the role specialists such as medical examiners play in solving crimes. Each title in the series demonstrates the ways a crime may be solved, from the various applications of forensic science and technology to the reasoning of investigators. Sidebars examine both the limits and possibilities of the new technologies and present crime statistics, career information, and step-by-step explanations of scientific and legal processes.

The Crime Scene Investigations series strives to be both informative and realistic about how members of law enforcement—criminal investigators, forensic scientists, and others—solve crimes, for it is essential that student researchers understand that crime solving is rarely quick or easy. Many factors—from a detective's dogged pursuit of one tenuous lead to a suspect's careless mistakes to sheer luck to complex calculations computed in the lab are all part of crime solving today.

"Taking in the Evidence, Doing the Work"

At 10 o'clock on the morning of July 19, 2004, Mark Douglas Hacking of Salt Lake City, Utah, called police to report that his pregnant wife, Lori, had not returned from her morning jog. Police investigated her disappearance and quickly became convinced that the Hacking apartment was not simply the missing woman's home. It was a crime scene. They found blood on the headboard and frame of the couple's bed. They found a brand new mattress and new bedding in the house, with receipts indicating they had been purchased that day. They also found a bloody knife stashed away in a drawer in the bedroom. As the search widened, they discovered a cut-up mattress that matched the couple's box spring in a trash bin near Mark Hacking's work.

Hacking was arrested even before Lori's remains were found in the Salt Lake City landfill in October 2004. Upon the discovery, Assistant District Attorney Robert Stott stated, "We were confident we could go forward with the case without a body, and now we have the body."[1]

The Lori Hacking murder is only one of about 16,000 homicides that take place in the United States each year. Although the numbers sound large, they have been higher in the past. The U.S. Department of Justice recorded 18,980 murders in 1985 and 24,530 in 1993. The latest figures, for the year 2004, were 16,137. These deadly incidents range from murders involving spouses to those committed by serial killers, from drug-related homicides to deadly clashes between neighbors over fairly minor disputes.

Many of the cases are quickly wrapped up, but about six thousand go unsolved every year. One of the most notorious in the latter category is the murder of child beauty queen JonBenet

An assortment of firearms, bagged as evidence after a series of raids, forms part of the crime-solving trail.

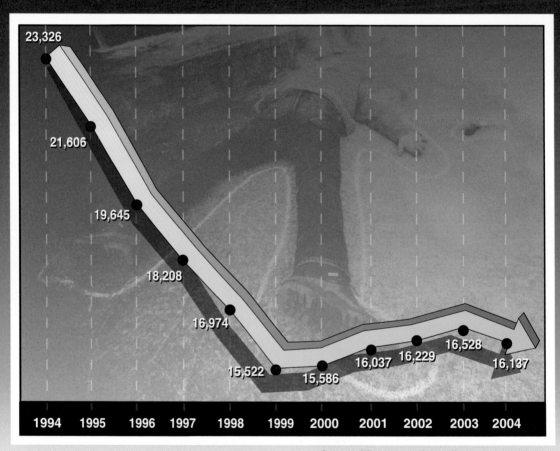

Downward Trend in Homicides in the United States

23,326

21,606

19,645

18,208

16,974

15,522

15,586

16,037

16,229

16,528

16,137

1994 1995 1996 1997 1998 1999 2000 2001 2002 2003 2004

Source: FBI,Uniform Crime Reports, 1994-2004

Ramsey, who was found dead in her home in Boulder, Colorado, the day after Christmas in 1996. A ransom note and DNA (deoxyribonucleic acid) evidence were found at the crime scene, but no guilty party has yet been identified. In October 1999 Tom Wickman, the twenty-two-year veteran of the Boulder police department who helped lead the investigation, stated, "This [inability to solve the case] has been frustrating to our people, to our city and to people around the country. . . . Life is not always fair. But giving up is not an option. You don't quit; you can't."[2]

"Science Is Great"

When it comes to investigating modern-day murders like those of Lori Hacking and JonBenet Ramsey, crime scene investigators rely on a variety of practices and procedures. These include gathering eyewitness testimony, checking alibis, determining motives, and running background checks of suspects' criminal histories. One of the most vital aspects of any investigation, however, is the processing and analysis of forensic evidence, evidence that helps police and the courts develop an understanding of a crime and bring the perpetrator to justice.

Forensic science plays a much larger role in solving murders today than it did in previous decades. Personal computers, advanced lab equipment, and DNA profiling have not only made scientific analysis more effective but are allowing experts to find solutions to murders that would have looked hopelessly unsolvable twenty years ago. "DNA technology has changed so much in the last 10, even five years. It is so much better now," homicide detective Frank Merriman of Los Angeles says. "The more advanced it gets the more cases we solve. Science is great."[3]

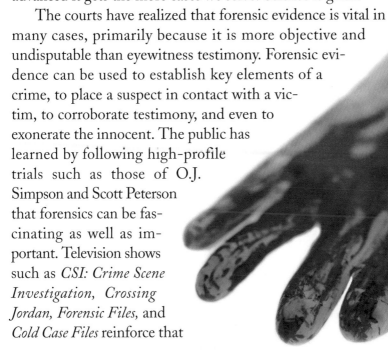

A bloodstained glove can be a crucial piece of evidence.

The courts have realized that forensic evidence is vital in many cases, primarily because it is more objective and undisputable than eyewitness testimony. Forensic evidence can be used to establish key elements of a crime, to place a suspect in contact with a victim, to corroborate testimony, and even to exonerate the innocent. The public has learned by following high-profile trials such as those of O.J. Simpson and Scott Peterson that forensics can be fascinating as well as important. Television shows such as *CSI: Crime Scene Investigation*, *Crossing Jordan*, *Forensic Files*, and *Cold Case Files* reinforce that fascination. As author Jon Zonderman notes, "In almost every police drama, there is at least one episode . . . where the police have a significant encounter with the scientific sleuths. These are often well-scripted segments that . . . serve to teach the public about the work done in the back office."[4]

A Team Effort

By watching forensic shows, the public has also learned that, when it comes to murder, there are few lone geniuses such as Sherlock Holmes or Columbo who solve a case on their own. Rather, tracking down a perpetrator involves numerous individuals with a variety of backgrounds. Some work with evidence that ranges from blood to bugs to ballistics. Some specialize in fields such as anthropology, psychology, and medicine. Those who process a crime scene—collect fingerprints, find bloodstains, pick up hair and fiber, and the like—have different responsibilities from those who analyze such evidence in the lab. Each is important in his or her own way, however, as forensics expert Barry A.J. Fisher writes: "Each person has a vital role to play and each element must be accomplished in a responsible, professional and timely manner to make every component function properly. Each one working on a case should feel that he or she is essential to the successful completion of an investigation."[5]

No matter where an investigation leads, the beginning is always the "scene of the crime," as mystery writers like to call it. Whether that scene is a bedroom, a shopping mall, a desert, or a mountainside, the experts have to collect and process every bit

Investigators have used DNA, represented by this model of the double helix, to solve thousands of crimes.

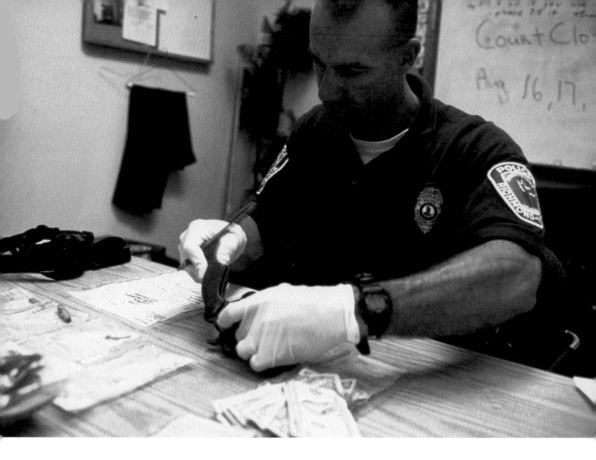

of evidence they can find and then try to make sense of the crime. That is their job, and they find it rewarding despite its dark overtones. Forensic expert Calum Price explains: "There's such satisfaction in taking in the evidence, doing the work, and knowing you've found the right answer. . . . It's just terribly satisfying to take all that uncertainty, the chaos of a crime scene, and put it all back together in one coherent story. Ya gotta love that!"[6]

A federal agent processes evidence, including money and a gun, in the crime lab.

CHAPTER 1

The Crime Scene

On May 28, 1981, Milwaukee, Wisconsin, police were called to the home of thirty-year-old Christine Schultz, whose two sons found her shot to death in her bedroom. Officer Stuart Honeck, who was also Schultz's boyfriend, was among the first to arrive at the crime scene. He discovered Schultz lying on her bed, her hands bound with cord, and a bullet hole in her back.

After making certain that she was dead, the officers took photos, but let two hours pass before calling the medical examiner to examine the body. During that time, they removed the cord from Schultz's hands, wrapped her body in plastic, and searched the house. When the victim's ex-husband Elfred Schultz—also a police officer—arrived, they allowed him to help search the home as well.

The handling of the Schultz crime scene is an example of what happens all too often in criminal cases: Locales are not protected until they can be properly investigated. In this case, the body was moved, so evidence on it was disturbed. The medical examiner was not called immediately, so he was hampered in his ability to accurately determine time, manner, and cause of death. Nonessential persons were also allowed in the home. No one knows if they touched surfaces or removed evidence, but according to the Locard Exchange Principle, formulated by French criminologist Edmund Locard, their very presence altered the scene. As forensic expert Michael Baden and his co-author Marion Roach write, "Enter, turn around and walk right out, touching nothing, and you have still left something of yourself behind—a grain of sand from the sole of your shoe, perhaps, or a fiber from the carpet of your car. It could be a hair—yours or that of someone you touched earlier."[7]

Investigators prepare to carefully analyze bloody sheets and a bloodstained walkway at the scene of a double murder.

"A Complex Puzzle"

A crime scene is some of the most complex territory in the world. It can be as small as a telephone booth or as large as a shopping mall. Although it encompasses everything on the site where the body was found, it is often more than just that locale. When a victim is killed in one place and dumped somewhere else, for example, there are two crime scenes for the single incident. If a victim is transported in a car, that car is a "scene" that has to be examined, too, as does any other spot where evidence might be found. Author and forensic expert N.E. Genge explains: "A 'crime scene' . . . is . . . the staging and planning areas, the paths of flight to and from the primary scene, and the paths between the primary and secondary scenes."[8]

Outdoor crime scenes are more difficult to process because perimeters are hard to define. An area may be taped off and secured, but if a piece of evidence turns up outside that area, boundaries have to be redrawn. In addition, at outdoor scenes, evidence can be blown away by the wind, covered by falling leaves, carried off by animals, or washed away by rain. The

Forensic scientist Dr. Henry Lee examines a bullet hole at the scene of a shooting.

Locard's Exchange Principle

Every crime scene investigator has heard of Locard's Exchange Principle, which holds that anyone entering or exiting a room changes it in some way. In his book Forensics for Dummies, *Douglas P. Lyle explains:*

Say that you [are a homemaker and] have two children and a cat. You run out to take care of some errands that include stopping at a furniture store, the laundry, and the house of a friend who has one child and a dog. From a forensics standpoint, this sequence of events can provide a gold mine of information. You leave behind a little bit of yourself at each stop, including:

- Hair from yourself, your children, and your cat.
- Fibers from your clothing and the carpets and furniture in your home and car.
- Fingerprints and shoeprints.
- Dirt and plant matter from your shoes.
- Biological materials, if you accidentally cut yourself and leave a drop [of blood] on the floor or sneeze into a tissue then drop it in a trash can.

But that's not all. You also pick up similar materials everywhere you go:

- Fibers from each sofa or chair you sat on at the furniture store ride away on your clothes, as do hair and fibers left behind by customers who sat there before you.
- Fibers of all types flow through the air and ventilation system and settle on each customer at the laundry.
- Hair from your friend, her child, and her dog latch on to you as you go away. You also collect fibers from your friend's carpet and furniture.
- Fibers and hairs that have fallen to the floor attach to your shoes and pants at each stop.
- Dirt, dust, plant material, and gravel are collected by your shoes everywhere you set foot.

In short, by merely running errands, you become a walking trace evidence factory.

killer may completely or partly bury the body, forcing investigators to carefully excavate it, while photographing each step and collecting soil samples and any nearby foreign material.

A body of water is one of the most challenging outdoor crime scenes to identify and process. Boundaries are literally

Processing a Murder Scene

1 Interview: One crime scene investigator interviews the first law enforcement officer at the scene and witnesses to determine what allegedly happened, what crime took place, and how the alleged crime was committed.

2 Examine: Investigators conduct an examination of the scene that includes identifying possible evidence, identifying points of entry and exit, and recording the general layout of the crime scene.

Photographers play a critical role in recording the details of the crime scene.

3 Photograph: A crime scene photographer takes pictures immediately and regularly throughout the investigation to compile a pictorial record of the appearance of the crime scene and possible physical evidence.

4 Sketch: A member of the team completes a rough sketch that depicts the layout of the crime scene, the exact position of the deceased victim, and the exact position of possible evidence at the scene.

5 Process: The crime team identifies, evaluates, and collects physical evidence from the crime scene for further analysis in the crime laboratory.

fluid. Evidence has usually washed away or dropped to the bottom and been covered in mud or sand. Divers often must be called in in such situations, and they can be hampered by cold temperatures and poor visibility. In the 1994 case of child murderer Susan Smith, for instance, even after she told police exactly where she had sunk her car with her two small sons inside, divers had to make two exhaustive attempts to find the automobile, which was located in eighteen feet of water in John D. Young Lake in South Carolina.

Fingerprints are usually taken with ink, although that may change in the near future.

In contrast to outdoor crime scenes, indoor scenes are easier to identify and process. Indoor locales are usually cleaner, more protected, and bounded by walls. Surfaces are smoother and harder, making blood, fingerprints, and the like easier to find and collect. Nevertheless, indoor scenes are still challenging, and if the body has been buried in a cellar, burned in a furnace, or dismembered and carried away, investigators may be faced with many of the same obstacles involved in processing an outdoor scene. Author and journalist David Fisher observes, "A crime scene is . . . a mystery waiting to be unraveled, a complex puzzle. . . . Anything found at a crime scene might provide the single clue needed to break the case."[9]

First Responders

Whether the crime scene is indoors, outdoors, or underwater, police are usually the first responders, and their first responsibility is securing the scene to preserve evidence that may be fragile. In the Schultz case, the first officer on the scene should have quickly cordoned off the house with yellow barrier tape and then concentrated on holding back news reporters, curious bystanders, and even law enforcement officials who wanted to get a first-hand look at what happened. Honeck and Schultz, who knew the victim and had the potential of being suspects, should certainly have been barred from entering the home. Crime scene investigators should have been the only ones to enter and examine the body. Barry Fisher reemphasizes the importance of a secure crime scene: "Errors committed in the protection and examination of the crime scene can never be rectified [fixed]. The eventual success of the investigation can thus be completely dependent upon the preventative and preliminary measures taken by the officer who first arrives at the crime scene."[10]

A New Hampshire crime scene investigator carefully gathers evidence at the scene of a murder.

In addition to securing the scene, a first responder's responsibilities include recording the names of witnesses and other persons who are on-site and keeping them separate from each other until they have been interviewed. First responders often coordinate with crime scene technicians to ensure that everyone at the crime scene is fingerprinted. Usually, this is done using an ink roller that is run over the fingertips, which are then pressed against a card. Jon Zonderman, however, predicts changes in the near future:

> [Soon]   fingerprinting with ink will be a thing of the past. . . . Already, hundreds of police departments are using "live scan" technology to take full sets of prints: Instead of rolling inked fingers on a pad, clean fingers are rolled over a glass

panel . . . to gain a full picture of the pattern. The print can be immediately seen on a computer screen to make sure the transfer is complete.[11]

Prints taken from on-site individuals who know the victim are referred to as elimination prints. They do not identify the murderer—although they could if he or she is present. Instead, they allow police to match prints with known individuals and highlight those unknown prints at the scene that need to be identified.

First responders must also note conditions that may change by the time the full crime team arrives. For instance, they should notice whether lights are on or off when a room is entered, whether any fumes or odors are present, and whether a room is unusually warm or cold. If such conditions are overlooked, later analysis can be impacted. In the 1985 murder of Ellen Sherman in the bedroom of her Connecticut home, for instance, the friend who found the body failed to tell the police that the air conditioning had been on and the bedroom was extremely cold when he entered it. He had immediately turned the air conditioner off. By the time the police and medical examiner arrived, the room was at a normal temperature, about 70 degrees. Unaware for a time that the colder temperatures had slowed the decomposition process dramatically, the medical examiner at first set the time of death later than the actual time of death. This played into the murderer's plan, in which he provided an alibi for himself for the believed critical time period.

Crime Scene Investigators

Investigators who process the crime scene commonly arrive on the heels of the first responders. In small towns, the crime team may be one or two police officers who carry out a multitude of investigative tasks between them. In cities, it is usually a group of individuals connected with the police or district attorney's office who process the locale and help uncover the truth of what took place there.

One of the most important members of the crime team is the photographer, who uses a variety of cameras and film to capture the scene. Clear photographs are vital once the crime scene has been secured, so everything is captured from several angles. Accompanying notes describe each shot to eliminate confusion or forgetfulness.

The body is photographed exactly as it was found from various distances. So too is anything else that seems relevant or suspicious. This could include blood spatter on walls, cigarette ashes on the floor, or a tiny shard of glass found under the vic-

Becoming a Crime Scene Investigator

Job Description:
A crime scene investigator reports on crime scenes and other significant events to systematically locate, identify, process, and collect physical evidence at the scene.

Education:
Most aspiring crime scene investigators need a bachelor's degree in biology, forensic science, or criminal justice.

Qualifications:
After completing their education, aspiring crime scene investigators should gain work experience in a medical examiner's office or police department. Additional personal qualifications include a logical and analytical approach to work; highly developed observational and scientific skills; objectivity while reaching critical conclusions; strong written and verbal communication skills; and the ability to perform well within a team.

Salary:
$20,000-50,000

Blood is only too common at a murder scene, but investigators work carefully with it because more than one person's blood may be present. In the O.J. Simpson case, for instance, blood from both murder victims, Nicole Brown Simpson and Ron Goldman, was found. In addition, a trail of blood left by a third person led away from the bodies.

The crime team must be skilled in identifying blood, since dried blood can sometimes appear brown, or, after several months, black or even greenish gray. If a killer has cleaned the scene thoroughly, it can be virtually invisible. Thus, if they suspect that blood is present, investigators may collect the contents of bathroom and kitchen drainpipes. They may swab tiny cracks between tiles or under the edges of vinyl flooring where blood

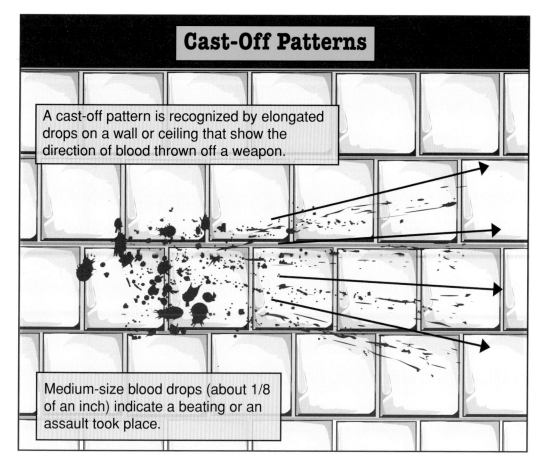

Cast-Off Patterns

A cast-off pattern is recognized by elongated drops on a wall or ceiling that show the direction of blood thrown off a weapon.

Medium-size blood drops (about 1/8 of an inch) indicate a beating or an assault took place.

By the Numbers

70

Percentage of 2004 murders in the United States that were committed with guns

may remain. If they are outside, they may bag samples of wet-looking soil for later analysis.

They may also use chemicals to bring invisible traces to light. One such chemical is luminol. When sprayed on a surface in the dark, luminol reacts with hemoglobin (an iron-containing pigment in red blood cells) and causes it to glow bluish green. The luminol test is not always accurate, however. Other substances, including household bleach, can also produce a glow. But, as author Tom Harris notes,

[Luminol] can reveal essential information that gets a stalled investigation going again. For example, hidden blood spatter patterns can help investigators locate the point of attack and even what sort of weapon was used. . . . Luminol may also reveal faint bloody shoe prints, which gives investigators valuable information about the assailant and what he or she did after the attack.[14]

Evaluating Blood Spatter

If investigators find blood spattered around the room, they may call in a blood pattern expert to help them analyze what the spatter signifies. Crime scene technician Daryl W. Clemens notes, "A great deal of specialized knowledge is required for the proper interpretation of blood stain patterns. Without this knowledge the investigator may not even know what he needs to document, let alone how to do it."[15]

Among other things, blood spatter experts know that blood hits a surface in a characteristic way. Drops that fall straight down onto a surface are circular, while those that hit at an angle are elongated with a point. Thus, when a wounded person is running, he or she is likely to leave a trail of elongated

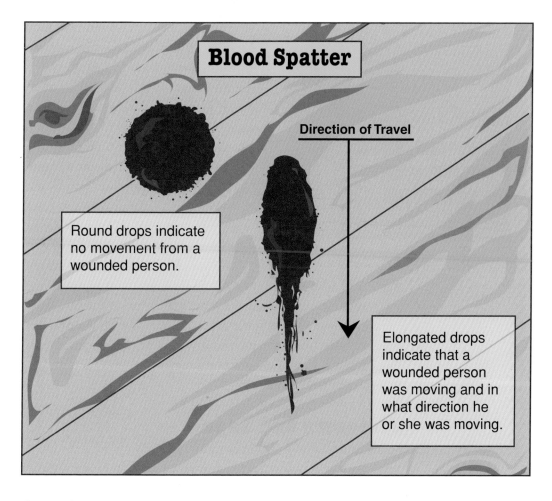

drops of blood, the point of which can indicate the direction of travel.

Such a trail of blood is commonly defined as low-velocity spatter and is characterized by large drops that are relatively few in number. A fine mist of blood droplets on a surface is defined as high-velocity impact spatter. Such a mist is created when a bullet strikes a victim. Medium-velocity impact spatter—a spray of medium-size drops—is commonly associated with something like a beating or a similar type of assault. Spurted lines of blood drops on a wall and/or ceiling of a room are recognized as "cast-off patterns," blood thrown off a weapon such as a knife or a crowbar while it was being used to strike the victim.

6

Number of quarts of blood in the human body

Although a large amount of blood at a scene might seem confusing to the untrained eye, blood spatter experts see the scene as a puzzle that can eventually be solved. Using their experience aided by geometric formulas, preprinted tables, and computers, they reconstruct the violent event to prove or disprove scenarios put forth by defense and prosecution lawyers. Such was the case with the Yvonne Mathison murder in Hawaii in 1992. Mathison's husband claimed that she was killed after she jumped out of their van on a highway and was struck by a car. Blood spatter evidence inside the van, however, clearly told criminologist Henry Lee that Yvonne had been struck while sitting in the driver's seat. This not only disproved her husband's story but caught him in a lie that ultimately sent him to prison.

Tweezers and Tape

In addition to collecting blood and other biological evidence, investigators go over the room with magnifying lenses, tweezers, tape, and small vacuum cleaners with special filters to collect soil, fiber, and hair. When collecting such evidence—known as trace evidence—the team must use their instincts and common sense in order to know what to ignore and which innocent-looking items might be significant in the investigation. Forensic consultant and author Jon J. Nordby explains:

> You have to know how to use your experience and reasoning to distinguish evidence from coincidence. . . . Part of this skill is the ability to think rationally and make distinctions among many variables in order to interpret what specific things mean at a crime scene. In other words, you know whether you should go through

a trash basket, pick up a stray thread, check beneath fresh paint, or preserve the hair on someone's brush.[16]

Even the most mundane items sometimes prove crucial at a later date. For instance, a photo receipt collected from serial killer John Wayne Gacy's wastebasket proved that a young boy police were looking for had been in Gacy's home. This led investigators to perform a more thorough search and ultimately find the bodies of the more than thirty young men and boys Gacy had killed and hidden in the crawl space under his house between 1972 and 1978.

As evidence is discovered, it must be packaged, so the crime team carries a variety of cardboard boxes, paper bags, bindles (paper envelopes), vials, and small bottles with lids. Very small items such as individual hairs, fibers, and shards of glass are first folded in a sheet of clean paper and then placed in a clean bindle or envelope. Each item of clothing, sheet, or towel is placed in its own paper bag to prevent cross-contamination. If something is wet with blood or some other substance, it is air-dried before packaging to prevent the growth of bac-

Human hairs coated with blood are bagged and labeled for later analysis.

teria or mold. If time or space does not permit this, the damp object is placed in a clean plastic container and dried immediately upon arrival in the crime lab. Items bearing fingerprints are se-cured individually in separate boxes so that the prints will not be smudged. The same is true for items bearing shoe and tire prints, or casts of such prints.

In addition to careful packaging, the crime team must label each item and state what it is, where it came from, and who packaged it. This is the first step in creating a chain of custody, a record documenting that all evidence has been maintained correctly in case it is

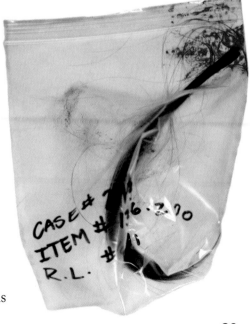

CASE #
ITEM # 16·2·10
R·L·

needed later in court. To create a valid chain, each person who has contact with the evidence must sign the tag and the evidence log that goes with it. Such a log shows that the evidence is always in the care of a qualified person. If a chain of custody is not maintained properly, valuable evidence can be deemed inadmissable in court.

Evidence must be transported in a timely manner to the crime lab. In the O.J. Simpson case, the prosecution was unable to win a conviction in part because vials of blood that were collected at the crime scene were left in a hot van for hours. The defense argued that this resulted in degradation of the samples. Moreover, incomplete documentation of who had controlled the samples and insinuations that tampering might have occurred gave jurors room for reasonable doubt and Simpson was acquitted.

The O.J. Simpson murder case was fascinating to police and the public because it occurred in a well-to-do neighborhood and involved a high-profile suspect. To those professionals who

During his trial for murder, O.J. Simpson shows jurors gloves similar to a pair found at the crime scene.

Forensic scientist Dr. Henry Lee describes the processing of bloodstains during the O.J. Simpson trial.

analyze evidence in crime labs across the country, however, evidence from high-profile murders is viewed no differently than objects taken from other crime scenes. This is because they know they are obligated to uncover the truth connected with each and every piece of evidence they receive. That knowledge makes everything from chunks of cement walls to grains of pollen important and compelling. FBI forensic chemist Kelly Hargadon notes, "[The evidence is] always something different. . . . You never know what it might be. When I open up a case for the first time it's as exciting as opening up a present."[17]

CHAPTER 2

Under the Microscope

After investigators carry out a careful and thorough examination of the crime scene, most evidence is analyzed in order to glean all the information it has to offer about the victim and the killer. That further analysis is carried out in the crime laboratory, where chemists, technicians, and others have the time, space, and equipment necessary to scrutinize even the most minute pieces.

Some of the most important evidence to be inspected is trace evidence—small, often microscopic material that may appear insignificant to the untrained eye but can be an important means of catching a killer. Forensic experts Max M. Houck and Ken Wiggins write, "Often characterized as . . . evidence that only weakly associates the suspect, victim and crime scene, trace evidence is so much more. DNA, despite the public and professional accolades [praise], only answers the question 'Who?' Trace evidence may be able to tell you 'what, where, how and when.'"[18]

The Crime Lab

There are more than three hundred city, county, state, and federal crime labs in the United States. Some are small and underfunded. Some are state-of-the-art units complete with computers, electron microscopes, lasers, other scientific instruments, and a well-trained staff. Many are linked to state law enforcement agencies. Others are under the direction of a district attorney's office, and a few are administered by universities. Over two hundred are accredited by the American Society of Crime Lab Directors Laboratory Accreditation Board (ASCLD/LAB), an organization dedicated to providing excellence in forensic science analysis.

A San Diego police department crime lab specialist peers into a comparison microscope, one of many sophisticated tools used for analyzing trace evidence.

The FBI Forensic Laboratory, Quantico, Virginia

5,000
Number of guns the lab possesses that can be disassembled to provide spare parts to test-fire damaged weapons that might have been used in a crime

1,200
Number of DNA samples the lab can process annually

250,000
Number of fingerprints the lab can process annually

1.4 MILLION
Number of convict profiles in the lab's DNA database

The most prestigious crime laboratory in the country to-day is the FBI crime laboratory, which was established in 1932 in Washington, D.C. and is now located adjacent to the FBI Academy in Quantico, Virginia. The FBI lab has departments specializing in firearms, tool marks, hairs and fibers, latent fingerprints, and DNA analysis. The lab also houses a chemistry/toxicology unit, a photography unit, and a materials analysis unit, among others. Every day, examiners there receive more than six hundred pieces of evidence—everything from specks of paint to human skulls. Despite the volume, they give everything careful consideration, and charge nothing for their work. David Fisher notes, "The FBI lab was established to provide impartial investigative services for all federal agencies in criminal and civil matters, and all local and state law enforcement agencies in criminal matters, and to do so absolutely free of charge. There is never a fee for requesting an examination. This is America's crime lab."[19]

Whether prestigious or unremarkable, all crime labs have one thing in common: They are places where people work to find solutions to crimes. Everything done there is done for a practical purpose. According to Fisher, "The crime lab is that place where science meets murder. It's where the wonders of modern science and space-age technology are used to transform clues into hard evidence."[20]

A lock of hair may provide important information about a crime.

Analyzing Trace Evidence

When crime lab analysts begin their work in crime laboratories across the country, they generally focus on the most easily lost or destroyed material, much of which is trace evidence, such as hair, fibers, metal filings, building materials, pollen and spores, cosmetics, soot, and a host of other things. Fisher explains, "A

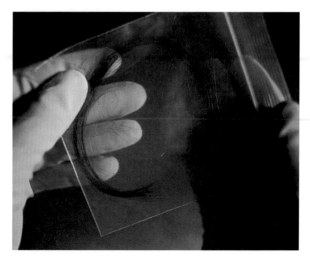

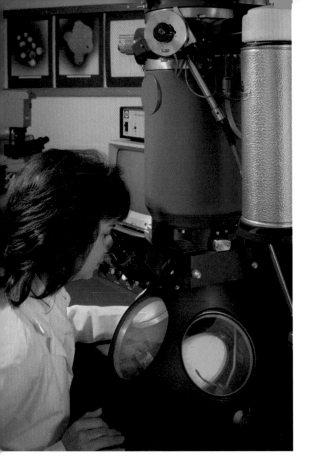

An electron microscope allows forensic scientists to see the particles that make up objects.

blood-soaked shirt might be sent to DNA for the primary investigations, but even before looking at it, the DNA examiner will send it to Hairs and Fibers because hairs and fibers fall off easily and important evidence might be lost."[21]

Great care must be taken when working with trace evidence. FBI crime lab analyst Jim Corby says, "If we handle it carelessly or touch it the wrong way it might literally jump across the room. A breeze from an air vent can blow away the most important evidence in a case. At one time or another probably every person in this unit has been down on his knees searching the floor for a chip of paint."[22]

Because trace evidence is so minute, specialized equipment is used in the lab to analyze it. Various types of microscopes are invaluable. In addition to the traditional compound microscope, which uses light reflected and magnified through a series of lenses, the comparison microscope is extremely effective as well. The comparison scope is actually two microscopes joined by a crosspiece that ties them together. Using it, two objects can be viewed at the same time, allowing a person to easily note differences and similarities.

Another type of microscope, the stereoscopic microscope, has double eyepieces and double lens systems that provide three-dimensional images. Stereoscopes are valuable for examining odd-shaped evidence. So are electron microscopes, which are found in the best-equipped labs. These scopes use a beam of highly energized electrons (subatomic particles) to examine specimens and gain information regarding their structure and composition. Electron microscopes can magnify objects up to 100,000 times and thus can reveal the tiniest surface features, as well as the shape, size, and arrangement of parti-

As Good as Gold

Although undervalued by some, paint evidence can sometimes be crucial in solving a case. Author David Fisher gives an example in his book Hard Evidence.

When a ten-year-old Los Angeles boy was killed by a hit-and-run driver, his clothing was sent to the lab. It was processed in an airtight scraping room and carefully scraped with a metal spatula. Several tiny sparkling paint chips fell from his pants, perhaps having been held there by the boy's dried blood. Using the [lab's] paint file, these chips were identified as a gold metallic acrylic paint used on three car models by the same manufacturer. The lab reported to the Los Angeles Police Department [LAPD] that the killer would be driving one of these models.

It didn't take the LAPD long to discover that one of the boy's neighbors drove a gold sports car. The suspect claimed he had recently replaced the hood of his car because it had been damaged in a traffic accident. When the [original] hood was recovered and submitted to the lab, examiners were not only able to match the paint chips found in the victim's clothes to the car, they also found fibers caught in the metal that could be matched to the boy's jacket. Faced with the evidence, the owner of the car confessed to the crime.

cles making up the object. They can also provide information about the elements and compounds the object is composed of.

The "Workhorse of a Crime Lab"

Side by side with microscopes, the gas chromatograph (GC) and mass spectrometer (MS) are vital pieces of equipment in most up-to-date labs. Forensic psychologist and author Katherine

Ramsland writes, "The real workhorse of a crime lab is the gas chromatograph with mass spectrometry (GC/MS). Most things encountered at a crime scene are complex mixtures and with this method can be separated into their purest components."[23]

The gas chromatograph, which is used to separate the elements of an unknown substance, is like a high-intensity oven in which a liquid sample of an unknown is introduced, vaporized into a gas, and then funneled through a coil-shaped structure lined with chemicals. The various elements in the gas travel at different speeds through the structure, with small molecules traveling faster than larger ones. Gas chromatography can be compared to a race where everyone begins at the starting line but crosses the finish line at different times.

After passing through the GC, the newly separated elements can be placed in a mass spectrometer, which is used to measure their amounts. In the MS, molecules are separated according to their different masses (comparable to their weight) and then counted; the numbers are then sent to a computer. There, a graph of the number of particles with different masses is created. This is known as the mass spectrum.

Gas chromatography and mass spectrometry can lead to the identification of even the most barely discernible trace evidence ranging from poisons to drugs to explosives. In 2001, for instance, a Florida medical examiner, William Sybers, was found guilty of murdering his wife after an analysis of her tissues by GC/MS revealed the residue of succinylcholine, an uncommon, hard-to-detect paralyzing drug, in her embalmed tissues.

Information comes from many sources, including a microscopically enhanced cross-section of a hair root and follicle.

Fiber and Hair

With microscopes and GC/MS to help them examine a wide range of trace evidence, investigators regularly focus on fiber and hair, found at many crime scenes. Hair and fibers are not considered the strongest evidence to link killer and victim because they are "class characteristic" rather than unique to each individual. For instance, carpet fibers found at a murder scene might be traced to a suspect's car, but a defense lawyer could argue that the same type of fiber could also be found in thousands of other cars of the same make and model.

If other kinds of evidence connect a suspect to a crime, however, the presence of matching fibers or hairs can help build a strong circumstantial case against the person. And, as Ramsland observes, future scientific developments such as fiber computer databases may soon make more precise detection possible: "As forensic science advances with computers and increasingly more accurate means of detecting the component parts of small samples, trace evidence may soon play even more significant roles."[24]

The first step in fiber analysis is to compare color and diameter. Color is often analyzed using the microspectrophotometer, a combination of a microscope and a spectrophotometer (an instrument that helps identify a substance by directing a beam of light at it and obtaining what is known as its absorption spectrum). The microspectrophotometer produces a precise "fingerprint" of the dyes used. For other aspects of the examination, however, analysts use microscopes. They can reveal the size and nature of fibers. Cotton fibers look like blades of grass, for instance. A strand of wool is round, covered with scales, and honeycombed internally. Synthetics such as rayon or polyester are smooth and made of long, uniform chains of molecules called polymers.

Forensic scientists look for distinctive features in fibers. A magnified view of cotton fibers appears here.

Analysts also look for characteristics that might make the fiber distinctive: an unusual shape, lengthwise striations, pits on a surface, and so forth. With cords and ropes, they also look for such things as the number of strands or braids, the pattern of twists and turns of the strands, and the presence of any distinctive fibers. When comparing an unknown sample of fiber or cord with a known one, they are willing to say the two are consistent only if all points of comparison match.

When hair is found at the scene, analysts look at its cuticle (the tough covering of the hair shaft) and its cortex (the part that carries particles of pigment that give hair its color). This can help them determine if the hair is from an animal or a human, and if human, where it came from the body. Hair from the head is generally longer than other body hair. Pubic hair is coarse and curly. Facial hair is short and blunt. Analysts are also able to tell from a hair's size and shape whether it came from someone who is Caucasian, African, or Asian. Other information, such as whether the hair has been bleached, dyed, or otherwise treated, can be revealed under the microscope, too. A hair can reveal the presence of fleas or lice. It can testify that a victim ingested poison at some time, and the presence of a root can indicate that the hair was forcibly pulled out, perhaps during a struggle. At times, the owner's DNA profile can be determined from hair as well. Baden and Roach explain: "Plucked hairs include a root bulb containing cells with nuclei, which contain two strands of DNA."[25]

Dirt and Dust

In addition to hair and fiber, trace evidence includes rocks, minerals, vegetation, glass, paint chips, asphalt, brick, cinders, and particles of dust or dirt gathered from the crime scene, found on a suspect's clothing, or lodged in an object such as a car tire. When viewed under a microscope, all are unique in some way and can reveal much about their origin.

In one murder case, the killer entered the victim's home through a bedroom window, leaving behind a footprint in a

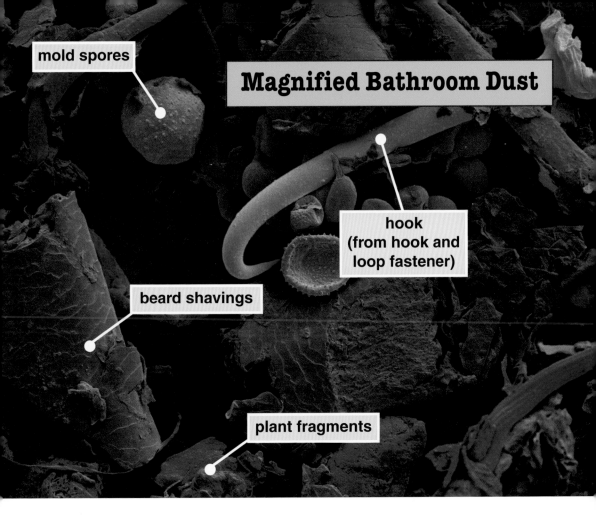

Magnified Bathroom Dust

mold spores

hook
(from hook and
loop fastener)

beard shavings

plant fragments

muddy flower bed below the window. When a suspect was arrested, police confiscated his muddy boots, which he claimed had become dirty when he was gardening in his backyard. Soil specimens submitted from the boots, the backyard, and the flower bed proved otherwise, however. Crime lab analysts found that one boot did carry soil that was microscopically similar to that in the suspect's yard, but mud from the other boot was not. Instead, it was microscopically consistent with the dirt from the victim's flower bed, proving that the suspect had stepped there in the recent past and then lied about his actions.

Microscopes are ideal for analyzing dirt samples. Color comparisons can be made under a comparison scope, which is also useful in determining the presence or absence of unique debris, rocks, and/or minerals. There are other forms of analysis that can be used, too. Density-gradient tests, for example,

An electron micrograph reveals a hidden world in a magnified speck of bathroom dust.

can provide more exact comparisons of the makeup of two samples. The test uses two long, narrow test tubes in which two liquids are layered in varying proportions such that each layer has a different density. When soil from the crime scene is placed in one tube, its components will sink to the layers corresponding to their own density values. Soil from the suspect's clothing, car, or shoes, placed in a second tube, will be processed in the same way. If the two tubes show the same density distribution, the two samples are considered a match, or coming from the same locale.

Glass, Paint, Rust

Glass is another type of trace evidence that can provide important clues for solving crimes. For instance, if a perpetrator smashes glass, some tiny slivers will adhere to that person's clothing even after that clothing has been cleaned, so those slivers will be found upon examination. Using a microscope, examiners are able to match that glass to glass found at the scene by measuring the density, color, thickness, and chemical composition of a shard. They also determine its refractive index by calculating the extent to which a beam of light is slowed as it passes through the glass.

A telltale pattern emerges in glass shattered by a bullet.

The identification of some kinds of glass is relatively easy because manufacturers keep records of the products they make. This is particularly true of automobile glass companies, since they are constantly providing replacements for all makes and models of cars. Forensic specialist Jay Paresh says, "Automobile glass, because you find it everywhere at accidents and hit-and-runs, is well-documented. In some cases, a piece of auto glass can narrow the possible vehicle to just one or two makes."[26]

Glass shatter patterns can also provide clues about how a murder took place. When working with shattered glass, examiners will often fit a broken pane together in order to analyze the pattern of fractures that caused it to shatter. For instance, when glass has been perforated by a bullet, the hole is narrow where the bullet goes in and wider in a crater pattern on the side where the bullet goes out.

In a slightly different manner than glass analysis, paint is broken down to its chemical constituents in order to be identified. Using gas chromatography and other techniques, crime lab investigators can determine the various pigments in a sample, the solvent that carries the pigment, the binder to make it stick to a surface, and additives to make it waterproof or shiny. They again turn to the microscope, however, to determine if the paint was applied with a brush, a roller, or a spray gun. They can tell in this way if it has been exposed to sun, rain, cigarette smoke, or cooking grease, too. With all that information, it is often relatively easy to match the sample back to its source.

As with glass, if paint evidence is believed to have come from a car, it can be compared with color samples in the National Automotive Paint File, which holds more than forty thousand samples. An analysis of automobile undercoat paint also helps narrow down possible manufacturers. When paired with a known make and model of a car, paint can often lead to a killer being apprehended. Such was the case in Arizona in 1984 when tiny specks of pink paint were found on the bumper of Frank Jarvis Atwood's pickup truck. Atwood was accused of striking eight-year-old Vicki Hoskinson with his pickup while she was riding

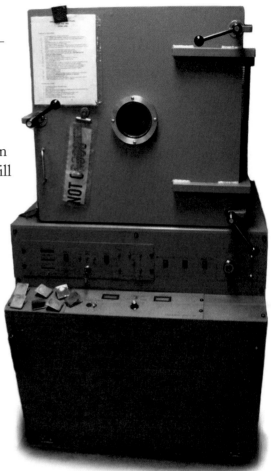

A few crime labs are equipped with vacuum metal deposition chambers, used to lift prints from plastic and non-porous materials.

her bike. He then took her into the desert and killed her. "It [the paint evidence] really wasn't more than a trace," FBI analyst Jim Corby remembered. "But it was enough to make a comparison."[27] Atwood was found guilty and sentenced to death in 1987.

Another kind of trace evidence—corrosion—is analyzed less often than paint, but it can prove helpful in forensic investigations, too. Corrosion can vary from flaky red rust on a crowbar to slimy algae buildup on a car dredged out of a river. And because experts know that items age differently according to their environment, they can tell how long an item has been in that environment by the thickness of the corrosion. They can tell other things as well. Finding a slimy, blackened gun in a lake that has a high sulfur content is reasonable, because sulfur creates black corrosion. If they find a rusty gun showing no speck of black in that same lake, however, they can state with certainty that it has been laying outside for a time but has not been in the lake for long. FBI metal specialist Bill Tobin explains further:

> If the corrosion I find on a submerged object isn't compatible with the environment, then I know we've got a problem. I know it probably hasn't been in that environment or hasn't been there for the period of time in question. But if everything is consistent, then the extent of the corrosion will give me a good idea how long it's been [there].[28]

Sticky Evidence

Trace evidence such as rust yields only a minimal number of clues in a murder investigation. Tape, however, can be a rich source of clues for crime lab analysts. In recent years, tape has become popular with perpetrators because it is strong, more difficult to loosen than rope, and is a quick way to bind a victim.

Investigators prefer its other qualities. They can easily determine what brand it is and trace it to its source. Its torn ends can sometimes be matched exactly to the end of a roll of tape

A Tree That Was a Murder Witness

Plants sometimes provide trace evidence that convicts murderers. In a 1993 case in Phoenix, Arizona, for instance, two seedpods from a palo verde tree were found in the truck bed of a murder suspect named Mark Bogan. Bogan's pager had previously been found near the nude body of a young woman who had been strangled. He had explained the pager's presence by claiming that he had picked up a female hitchhiker, they had gotten into an argument, and when he ordered her out of his truck she stole several items from his dashboard, including the pager. He denied killing her or being near the area where police found her body.

At the crime scene, however, detectives had noticed a clump of palo verde trees, one of which showed recent scratches on the bark. Using DNA analysis, a molecular geneticist at the University of Arizona matched the seedpods from Bogan's truck to the trees at the crime scene. The court admitted the plant DNA evidence at Bogan's trial, thus placing his truck at the crime scene. The jury convicted him of first-degree murder, and the conviction was upheld on appeal.

DNA evidence from a palo verde tree like the one pictured, linked the murderer to his crime in a 1993 Arizona murder trial.

45

found in a suspect's possession. Other trace evidence is often trapped in its sticky lengths as well. In one Canadian case, for instance, fibers from a suspect's gloves were recovered from the transparent packing tape used to bind a couple who were attacked and almost killed.

Sometimes, tape is the source of some of the most incriminating evidence that can be found at a crime scene. In the 1996 shooting of Rick Valdez in Tampa, Florida, a perpetrator was brought to justice after his fingerprint was found on electrical tape binding Valdez's arms and legs. And in a 2002 double homicide in Daytona Beach, Florida, a palm print on duct tape used to restrain one victim led to the arrest of an Orlando resident, Roy Lee McDuffie.

Plastic Links to a Crime

Like tape, garbage bags are another form of trace evidence that have become popular with killers in recent years. They are used for everything from smothering a victim to transporting body parts from the scene. Experts find them valuable because fingerprints, DNA, and body fluids can be retrieved off them. And if a bag found at a crime scene matches a roll of bags found in a suspect's possession, they can also be used to link that person to the crime.

To the untrained eye, all plastic bags on a roll look alike. Experts know, however, that such bags are produced sequentially (one after the other) on an assembly line where they are sealed and cut from one long line of plastic. During this assembly-line process, distinctive manufacturing irregularities regularly occur (for example, machinery picks up a stray hair or a speck of glue), and a sequence of bags will show that irregularity. These bags will also be boxed in the same sequence in which they were made. No other bags will have the same irregularity, so a bag from the series can be compared and matched to bags that were made directly before or after it.

In a case illustrating this circumstance, when a garbage bag containing a human arm was found in a city dumpster in Canada, police were able to match the arm to a missing apartment manager who lived nearby. Garbage bags containing the dead woman's possessions were also recovered from a nearby pawnshop. As the investigation progressed, police identified a suspect that lived in the dead woman's building. A box of plastic garbage bags was found in his apartment and were compared with the ones containing the remains and the woman's possessions. By matching irregularities in all the bags, examiners linked the suspect to the victim. He was convicted of second-degree murder.

Caught on Tape

Videotapes are a type of evidence that perpetrators seldom think about when carrying out their crimes. Nevertheless, these small strips of plastic, used for surveillance in banks, stores, ATMs, parking lots, and casinos, regularly help crime investigators by capturing images of robbers, kidnappers, and murderers. Some

Surveillance cameras, like these in Chicago, Illinois, sometimes capture crimes on tape.

A Louisiana forensic scientist, working on a sexual assault case, examines underwear for samples of DNA-rich semen.

police officers are even installing video cameras in their cruis-
ers in order to have a visual record of the individuals they interview while on patrol.

In one tragic case in Garrison, Texas, in January 1991, police officer Darrell Lunsford's video camera proved more useful than expected when it documented his own murder. With
the camera rolling, Lunsford stopped three men on a lonely
highway and tried to search their car for drugs. One of the men
grabbed Lunsford's gun, then shot and killed him. After the
men were apprehended, the tape played a large part in their
convictions.

Even when video recordings are of very poor quality with
images almost invisible due to worn-out recording heads,
scratched lenses, or inadequate lighting, skilled video analysts
are often able to clear up the images. They can get rid of in-
terference, lighten or darken images, and enlarge and sharp-
en blurry shots. The development of computer software that
looks for such problems and automatically corrects them makes
the job easier, too.

Because trace evidence rarely stands alone in convicting a
killer, experts like to find other forms of evidence to strength-
en the case. That is where biological evidence—blood and other body fluids—comes in. David Fisher points out, "There are
grand tales written in blood, tales of passion and horror and
murder, tales accessible only to those with the knowledge to
read them. It's the job of [a crime lab's] DNA Analysis Unit
to decipher these tales told by body fluids."[29]

CHAPTER 3

DNA, Blood, and Bones

When investigators come across biological evidence at the crime scene, they collect that evidence with particular care. Biological evidence consists of blood, saliva, bones, semen, and mucus, as well as insect and animal activity that may be connected with the murder. It also includes the body of the victim. Genge observes,

> So much evidence is found on and inside the human body that it constitutes a crime scene unto itself. After undergoing preliminary examination at the scene, a body is released into the hands of coroners or medical examiners, becoming the landscape that yet another rank of investigators will scrutinize intimately—right down to its basic molecules.[30]

The Autopsy

Murder victims can never verbally name their killers, but evidence in and on a body sometimes speaks louder than words. It is up to the medical examiner to bring that evidence to light during the autopsy process. An autopsy is a postmortem (after death) medical examination of the corpse, and is generally performed on anyone who suffered an unattended or suspicious death. Autopsies have several purposes: to determine the identity of the victim, the cause of death (bullet, rope, knife, etc.), the manner of death (accident, suicide, murder, natural causes, or undetermined), the mode of death (bleeding, ventricular fibrillation, etc.), and time of death. By uncovering the cause and manner of death, the medical examiner can usually

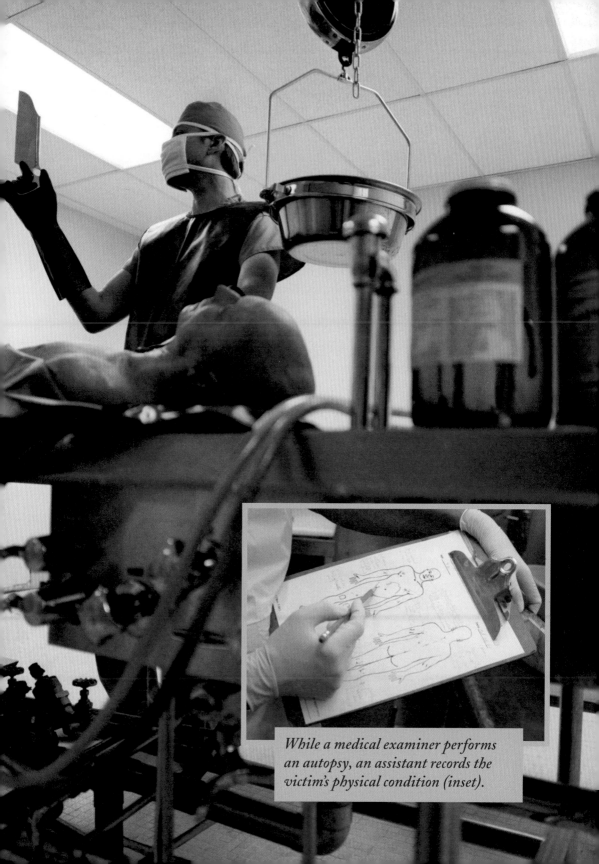

While a medical examiner performs an autopsy, an assistant records the victim's physical condition (inset).

Becoming a Medical Examiner

Job Description:

A medical examiner investigates sudden and unnatural deaths, performs autopsies, and conducts physical examinations and tests related to any matter of a criminal nature that is being considered by a court or district attorney. A medical examiner may be called on to perform forensic medical and pathology consultations, provide continuing education in the most current forensic investigative techniques and procedures to employees and law enforcement agencies, and testify in court to facts and conclusions disclosed by autopsies.

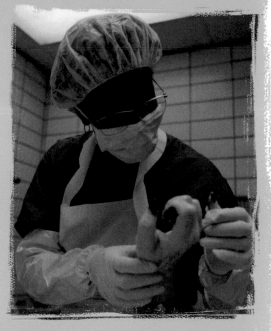

A victim's fingers undergo examination during an autopsy. Autopsies are one important job of a medical examiner.

Education:

After four years of college, an aspiring medical examiner must graduate from an accredited four-year medical school, complete a residency program in forensic pathology, and be licensed to practice medicine.

Qualifications:

As a physician, an aspiring medical examiner also needs to gain experience in forensic medicine, preferably by serving as an associate or deputy medical examiner. In some cases board certification in forensic pathology is required.

Salary:

$80,000-$180,000

suggest how a crime occurred. Sometimes reaching a conclusion is easy; at other times it involves a lengthy examination. "An average autopsy takes one to two hours," medical examiner Stanton Kessler states, "although I had one that involved fifty-four stab wounds that took two days."[31]

At the autopsy, medical examiners usually begin with a visual inspection of the body, noting every detail on a tape recorder as they go. They look at the color of hair and eyes. They also check the clothing, carefully remove it, and bag it for further examination. Trace evidence such as hair or fibers that may have come from the killer is collected as well. MEs then examine the hands and clip and save the fingernails, which may have the killer's blood or skin cells on them. The victim's hands are also swabbed for gunpowder residue. Hair is combed for evidence, and a few strands are collected. All body openings including ears, nose, genitalia, and so forth are checked for foreign objects. If sexual assault is suspected, a rape kit is used.

After X-rays of the body are taken, examiners take fingerprints and footprints. If the hands are dried and mummified, they sometimes inject liquid under the skin or soak the fingers for a time to rehydrate and soften the skin. They may simply take photos of the fingers if the skin is badly decomposed, or remove the skin from the fingertips and view it under a microscope. MEs also pay attention to any distinguishing marks such as birthmarks, scars, and tattoos. The latter sometimes provide the identity of an unknown victim. And according to Baden and Roach, "Some armed services tattoos may even include name, rank, and serial number."[32]

Lividity and Wounds

One of the most important things MEs look for is marks of lividity, also known as livor mortis. These are deep maroon discolorations under the skin where the blood pools as it settles into the lowest parts of the body after death. Lividity appears about two hours after death and does not change after about eight hours, so it shows how the body was resting for the period

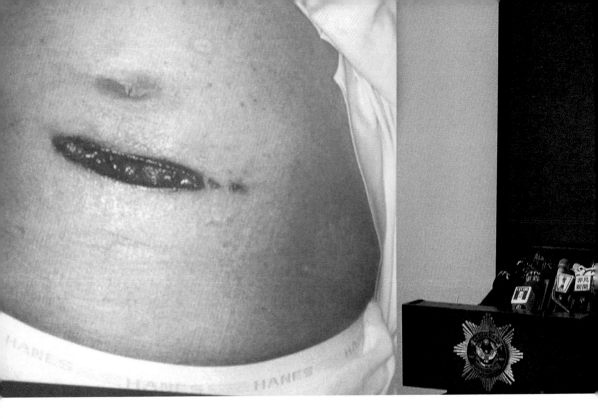

directly after death. If a corpse is found lying on its stomach but has lividity marks on its back, investigators know that it was moved sometime after death.

Examination of wounds is another vital part of the autopsy. MEs scrutinize and document all bruises, abrasions such as fingernail marks, crushing wounds such as hammer blows to the skull, and defense injuries (such as cuts to the insides of the hands, broken nails, and cut knuckles) incurred when victims tried to defend themselves. All knife wounds are studied in order to gain a general description of the weapon based on the wound's depth and shape. For instance, a circular wound would indicate a weapon such as an ice pick, while deep slits would indicate a large knife. Bullet holes are closely examined to determine if they are entrance or exit wounds (exit wounds are often larger), and the trajectory of the bullet is often tracked by following the path the bullet took through the body. MEs also look for gunpowder residue around the wound. A gun held directly against the skin creates a contact wound, leaving a "rim burn" around the opening (resulting from the heat and flare of the shot). By contrast, a gun held a few inches away produces a soot mark but no burn. Contact wounds sometimes leave the impression of the muzzle of the weapon on the victim's skin. A weapon held a few inches to a few feet away leaves "stippling," or tattoo like marks.

"Insects Are Everywhere"

If the body has been outdoors for any period of time, the medical examiner is likely to find insects or insect activity on it. In such a case, a forensic entomologist, a specialist that studies the behavior and life cycles of insects, is called in as early as possible—often at the crime scene itself—to evaluate such activity. Author and forensic investigator Katherine Steck-Flynn explains:

> Insects (arthropods) are everywhere. There are so many of them that each species has developed a unique niche in which to breed and feed. This is what the forensic entomologist hopes to take advantage of. Each species comes with a unique and predictable set of environmental conditions under which they can and will grow and thrive. To know the conditions in which a particular species will live is to know the history of the corpse they are living on or near.[33]

Neal Haskell is a highly regarded forensic entomologist.

Neal Haskell is one of the leaders in forensic entomology in the United States. He and students under him study every aspect of insect behavior in a spacious outdoor laboratory located near his home in Rensselaer, Indiana. There, they use humanely killed pigs for subjects and observe as they decay and are overrun by insects under various conditions, such as wet, hot, submerged, and

Maggots, shown here in a museum exhibit, can reveal the secrets of the dead.

so forth. A ninety-pound pig resembles a human body in its fat distribution, cover of hair, and ability to attract insects and is thus a good subject for study.

When some insects arrive to feed and breed on the pigs, they are trapped and identified. Others are merely observed and their life cycles charted in detail. In order to have a complete picture, soil samples are also taken, temperatures are charted, and weather conditions are noted. Another U.S. forensic expert, William Bass, explains:

There are many factors that can affect how a body decomposes, but we found that the major two are climate and insects. When a person dies, the body begins to decay immediately, and the enzymes in the digestive system begin to eat the tissue. You putrefy, and this gives off a smell. Up until about two and a half weeks, one of the best ways to tell how long a body is dead is to look at the insect activity. The first of the critters to be attracted to a decaying body are the blowflies. They come along and lay their eggs, which hatch into maggots. The maggots then eat the decaying tissue in a fairly predictable way.[34]

Insects other than flies are attracted to corpses, too, and their presence can add to clues regarding the time of death. Hawaiian entomologist Lee Goff noted of one case he worked on in 1996 that the body was host to a variety of insects, including clerid beetles, hide beetles, and soldier flies. The latter were particularly helpful. "[Soldier flies are] pretty definitive for my time estimate because they let the body age for

about 20 days before coming in. And the ones I collected were
. . . between 9 and 11 days old."[35] From that, Goff placed the
time of death at twenty-nine to thirty-one days before the body
was discovered.

Insect activity can also be another way to tell if the body
was moved after death. For example, if a corpse is discovered
near water but shows evidence of hosting dermestidae—a type
of beetle that is found only in dry environments—investigators know they should look for another crime scene in a drier
locale, where they may find more clues regarding the murder.

Inside the Body

Once a visual exam of the body is complete, the medical examiner begins the internal inspection. The ME begins by laying the body on its back and making a Y-shaped incision across
the chest from shoulder to shoulder and
down the center of the torso to the pubic bone (the forward portion of the
hip bones).

A medical examiner inspects a brain during an autopsy.

After laying the torso open, the ME
then removes the organs, such as the
heart, lungs, liver, and kidneys. He examines and weighs them, and takes tissue samples for microscopic examination. He also takes blood samples, and
collects fluid from the lungs and blad-
der for analysis. Reproductive organs
are checked, and if a pregnancy is discovered, the fetus is examined as well.

After the stomach and intestines are
examined, the contents are collected
and sent to the lab for further analysis.
In many cases, stomach contents can be
useful in determining time of death, although someone must know when the
victim last ate in order to make such an

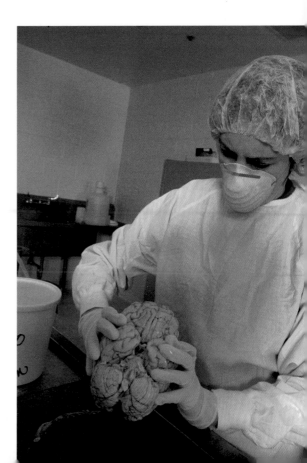

assessment. The ME also examines the victim's head inside and out, removing, weighing, and inspecting the brain and sectioning it for microscopic examination.

An analysis of the tissue samples as well as any evidence found in and on the body must be completed before the autopsy report can be written. This is often the time when the ME relies on the expertise of specialists in fields such as histology (the study of the microscopic structure of tissue), toxicology (study of poisons), serology (study of the properties and reactions of serums, especially blood serum), and pharmacology (study of drugs, including their composition, uses, and ef-

A forensic expert works to positively identify a murder victim by matching the victim's DNA with DNA from family members.

fects). Such specialists are able to determine through laboratory analysis of blood, tissues, and body fluids whether the deceased had drugs in the system; had been poisoned; or was HIV positive, had cancer, or had some other disease. When their analysis is complete, MEs will usually have a better notion of how and when the victim died, as well as any further investigative steps that need to be taken.

Genetic Fingerprints

In many cases, the medical examiner will order DNA analysis on some of the evidence found in or on the corpse, either to try to identify the victim or to link evidence to a suspect. DNA is genetic material that controls cellular function and heredity. Half comes from a person's father and half from the mother. DNA is present in the nucleus of all cells found in most body fluids—blood, semen, saliva, sweat, and mucus—as well as in hair and skin.

Microscopically, DNA resembles a long, spiraling ladder. It is composed of pairs of four nucleic acids—adenine, thymine, guanine, and cytosine—that are complex compounds made of purines, pyrimidines, carbohydrates, and phosphoric acid. Adenine always bonds with thymine, and guanine with cytosine. Baden and Roach explain, "Our genes are basically the biochemical directions spelled out by the specific sequence of pairs of these acids."[36]

Genes are composed of sequences of DNA, and, among humans, 99 percent of all genes are identical. The remaining 1 percent are the ones that contribute to human individuality, giving a person big ears, curly hair, flat feet, and so on. They are known as polymorphic because they are variable in shape. During DNA analysis, they serve as identifying markers because in no two persons (except identical twins) are all genes exactly the same.

To confirm the identity of a victim, samples of DNA are collected from relatives for analysis.

One of the procedures that crime lab chemists use to carry out DNA analysis is polymerase chain reaction (PCR). PCR, sometimes called molecular Xeroxing, is used to increase the amount of DNA available for testing when samples recovered at a crime scene are too small to test. PCR works by mimicking the cell's ability to replicate DNA. Using a vial and chemicals that unzip the double strands, chemists add the appropriate bases that will attach to opposite base pairs. N.E. Genge explains further: "The vial is first heated to about 160 [degrees]F for thirty seconds. This allows the two halves to unzip. When it is cooled to about 100F, . . . in less than half a minute, the process of duplication begins. The vial is reheated to

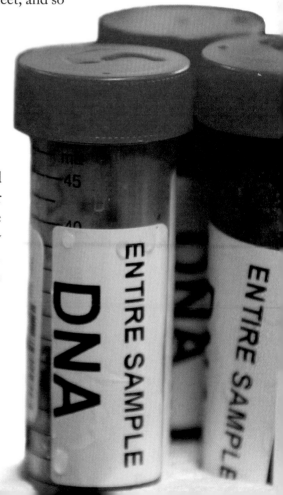

about 140F and duplication continues until both halves of the strand have been copied. The whole process takes about two minutes."[37] Using PCR, enough new DNA can be produced to be analyzed and profiled.

A recently developed procedure for analyzing DNA is known as short tandem repeat (STR). STR utilizes PCR technology to amplify and analyze sections of DNA that contain repeats of between one and five pairs of bases. These repeat segments, which occur in specific portions of the DNA, vary from person to person. Commonly, thirteen specific loci (locations) on a sample of DNA are examined and subsequently compared. The odds that two individuals will have the same thirteen-loci DNA profile are about one in a quadrillion—in other words, virtually impossible.

Solving Crimes with DNA

Genetic material is valuable because it is as unique as a fingerprint (except in the case of identical twins), survives longer than a fingerprint, and can be left on a variety of items at the crime scene by unwary killers. Barry Fisher notes, "You can get good DNA from a hatband or the nosepiece of a pair of glasses."[38]

The ability of crime lab investigators to use DNA as an identification tool, therefore, has had a revolutionary effect on solving murders. With the help of DNA analysis, cases in which there are no fingerprints, no smoking gun, and even no body can be solved. For instance, in 1988 blood found in fifty-eight-year-old Gregory Tu's home in Potomac, Maryland, was identified by DNA analysis as belonging to his missing companion, Lisa Tu, and Gregory was convicted of murder even though Lisa's body was not found. In 2002 Robert Pickton was arrested for the alleged murders of at least fifteen women based solely on their DNA found on his pig farm in British Columbia, Canada.

Investigators are also using mitochondrial DNA (mtDNA), or DNA found outside the nucleus of a cell, to identify murder victims and link killers to crimes. MtDNA can be found in bones, teeth, and hair and is typically passed only from mother to children, so there is little change in the mtDNA profile from generation to generation. This makes it a powerful tool. If a suspect is not available to match to DNA found at a crime scene, mtDNA from the suspect's mother or siblings can be assessed for identification purposes. Terry Melton, chief executive officer of Mitotyping Technologies in State College, Pennsylvania, one of a handful of laboratories in the United States that extracts cellular blueprints from evidence, notes, "It's [mtDNA analysis] been around for about 20 years. The armed forces used it to ID remains of Vietnam veterans for 10 years. Now it's being introduced quite a bit in court."[39]

Analysis of mitochondrial proteins (viewed with a specialized microscope) gives investigators a powerful crime-solving tool.

The success of DNA analysis in solving crimes has also motivated many law enforcement agencies throughout the United States to establish a national DNA data bank, where specimens from criminals can be stored and accessed. The FBI created the Combined DNA Index System (CODIS) in 1990, which tied together fourteen local and state DNA laboratories. In 1998 the FBI expanded CODIS to include a National DNA Index System (NDIS). The number of participating laboratories quickly grew to represent all fifty states, the District of Columbia, and Puerto Rico.

Today, CODIS enables forensic labs across the country to electronically exchange and compare DNA profiles from known violent offenders. As of March 2004 there have been 7,951 evidence-to-individual matches, which occur when DNA in blood or hair found at a crime scene matches DNA recorded in a data bank.

Reaching into the Past

Forensic experts are also using DNA analysis to track down killers from cases that have grown cold (are no longer being investigated) from lack of evidence. Since 1960, an estimated 200,000 such cases have accumulated nationwide.

One that was recently solved was the case of six-year-old Lisa Marie Bonham, who disappeared while visiting relatives in Reno, Nevada, in 1977. A day after her disappearance, Lisa's semen-stained clothing was found in a dumpster at a nearby highway rest stop, and her remains were later found scattered in the foothills of the Sierra Nevada. The technology of the time could not identify the killer from the semen, so the case went unsolved for twenty-three years. By 2000, however, advances in DNA technology encouraged investigators to reopen the case and retest Lisa's clothing. That testing, plus access to computer files, led them to arrest sex offender Stephen Smith, who pled guilty to the murder.

Defense attorney Barry Scheck, who is also an expert on DNA, helped found the first Innocence Project.

DNA analysis is not only helping to catch and convict killers but also helping to exonerate individuals who were wrongly found guilty in the past. Attorneys Barry C. Scheck and Peter J. Neufeld are two of the foremost leaders in the effort to remedy such injustice. To that end, they established the Innocence Project at the Benjamin N. Cardozo School of Law at Yeshiva University in New York City in 1992. The project relies on volunteer lawyers and law students to review cases that are brought to their attention, and as of 2003 had succeeded in proving 132 times that DNA in hair, semen, blood, or other biological evidence found at the scene did not belong to the individual convicted of the crime. All 132 cases ended in exoneration.

By the Numbers

206

Number of bones in the human body

Inspired by the successes of Scheck and Neufeld, other innocence projects have been established across the United States. They consist of volunteer police officers, investigative reporters, defense attorneys, students, and professors who believe that one innocent person in prison is too many. "The DNA cases have been really important for the innocence projects, because they establish innocence with such scientific certainty,"[40] says Keith Findley, codirector of the Innocence Project at the University of Wisconsin School of Law. And Neufeld observes, "We started out with a very simple goal, and that is to walk innocent people out of prison. And what it has evolved into is nothing less than a new civil rights movement in this country."[41]

Bone Specialists

There are instances when time, weather, insects, and animals have eradicated DNA and any other evidence to be found on a corpse, leaving only a skeleton behind. When that happens, forensic anthropologists are called in. Stanley Rhine,

Reading the Bones

Forensic anthropologists—bone specialists—can glean the following vital information from an examination of bones even when there is little or no soft-tissue evidence for forensic pathologists to work with:

Sex: Female bones tend to be smaller and lighter than male bones. The female's pelvis is wider than the male's. Brow ridges and occipital condyles (bones at the base of the skull) are larger and heavier in the male.

Ethnicity: African, Asian, and Caucasian skulls differ in facial structure, especially in the size and shape of the the nose and eye sockets.

Age: The amount of cartilage left at the growth points gives an indication of the victim's age. Older people's bones often show signs of bone diseases like arthritis and wear on the joints.

Height: A complete skeleton can be measured. With partial skeletons, investigators calculate the victim's height using formulas based on the length of long bones such as the tibia (shinbone), femur (thighbone), and humerus (upper arm bone).

Body type: Formulas based on bone characteristics are used to determine whether the victim was of light, medium, or heavy build.

professor emeritus in the Department of Anthropology at the University of New Mexico, explains: "In those cases in which soft tissue has been degraded by time, temperature, environment or other external forces, the only tissue remaining more or less intact is bone. The obvious person to call in to evaluate such material is the bone specialist."[42]

Forensic anthropologists can determine much information from bones. They can estimate age by looking at joint wear, which is greater in older people than in younger ones. The skull also gives an indication of age; sutures (where the bones join) continue to close throughout life, so a smooth skull indicates an older person. Sex can be determined by looking at pelvic bones, which are lower and wider in women and narrower in men. Height and body type can be estimated by measurements of the long bones in the legs; weight and muscularity can be determined by the size of bony protuberances where muscles attached.

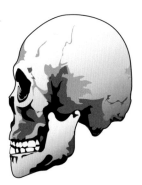

Asian

Anthropologists can sometimes read the story of how a victim died in his or her bones. Bullets leave holes in skulls, and knives nick ribs as they penetrate the body. A crushed larynx indicates strangulation. Horizontal cut marks on the jawbone show an effort to behead a person. Burned or charred bones show that the victim was in a fire.

Bones can even be used to identify a victim. The decayed body of Lori Hacking was identified when her teeth were matched to her dental records. In the case of serial killer John Wayne Gacy, law enforcement officials who could not identify over half of the bodies of his victims turned to forensic anthropologists Charles P. Warren and Clyde C. Snow. Warren and Snow first sorted and separated individual bones found piled under Gacy's home. They then examined them and compiled a chart for each skull and skeleton, based on thirty-five points of reference that could be

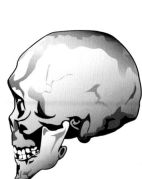

African

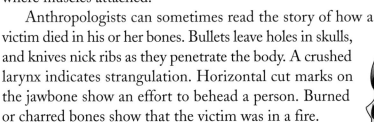

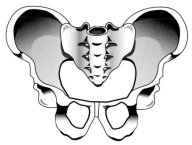

Female Pelvis

Male Pelvis

Caucasian

compared with descriptions in the many missing-person reports they had at their disposal. They were eventually able to identify numerous skeletons, including one of a five-foot-eleven, left-handed man exhibiting evidence of an old head injury and a broken left arm—a missing former marine named David Talsma.

Killers often leave only the slimmest of clues for experts to unravel when it comes to murder, but in some cases, they leave impressions—fingerprints, footprints, bite marks, and the like—that are plain for all to see. Genge writes, "Cheap, immutable, definitive—they're the sort of evidence every detective wants to have in hand when a case goes to trial. No wonder [prints] are major exhibits in so many trials, and that their collection, filing, and retrieval are integral aspects of crime scene processing."[43]

CHAPTER 4

Impressions of a Killer

Forensic investigators are always on the lookout for impression evidence, or prints relating to the killer left at the crime scene. They are familiar with fingerprints, which have helped solve murders for decades, and have become adept at recognizing and analyzing footprints, bite marks, tire impressions, and tool marks. They also have to be ready to identify and analyze unique kinds of impressions, however. In the case of the murder of Aimee Willard, a Pennsylvania teen who rolled under a car in an attempt to escape her killer in 1996, analysts helped solve the case by matching burn impressions on her side to markings on an oil pan on the underside of the killer's car. Willard had been burned by the hot metal before she had been caught and killed. Crime scene investigator Mike Byrd emphasizes, "Impression evidence is simply where . . . objects are pressed or stamped against one another allowing the objects to transfer and retain characteristics from one another. . . . Extreme patience and common sense are [sometimes] needed to find and recover these impressions."[44]

Loops, Whorls, and Arches

Impression evidence is always gathered at the crime scene, but the lab is the best place to develop and analyze much of it, particularly fingerprints. Fingerprint analysis begins by establishing whether the fingerprint has enough detail to be compared with those of a suspect and victim of the crime. The examiner determines if the fingerprint pattern is in the shape of a loop, whorl, or arch. Then the examiner compares the fingerprint to known fingerprints of the suspect and victim. The minute details of the print are compared, and if sufficient corresponding

Fingerprint Patterns

Fingerprints are a foolproof method of identification because each person's fingerprints are unique, and fingerprints do not change throughout a person's lifetime. Fingerprint ridges appear in three pattern types: loops, whorls, and arches.

Loops

The most common type of fingerprint pattern, loops begin at one side of the fingertip, double back, and exit on the same side.

Radial Loop
(Flows toward thumb)

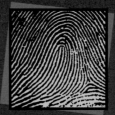

Ulnar Loop
(Flows toward little finger)

Whorls

Whorls are the second most common type of fingerprint pattern. They form a circular pattern which sometimes resembles a bull's-eye on a dartboard.

Plain Whorl

Double Looped Whorl

Arches

Arches are less common than loops or whorls. They form a wavelike pattern which begins on one side of the fingertip and ends on the other.

Plain Arch

Tented Arch

detail is observed between the print and one of the suspect's known prints, the examiner can conclude that the fingerprint from the crime scene was caused by that suspect. The process can be a long one because evidence fingerprints are often faint or smudged.

Since 1972, fingerprint searches have been expedited by the Automated Fingerprint Identification System (AFIS), which contains thousands of fingerprints that have been entered into computers by the FBI and other law enforcement agencies across the country. After a fingerprint examiner inputs the print, AFIS searches through its files for a match. In a matter of minutes it retrieves prints of known criminals that are similar to the sample entered. The examiner then makes a final, point-by-point visual comparison of all the prints using handheld magnifying glasses or comparison microscopes.

A San Diego Police Department fingerprint examiner studies the results of a database search.

If a fingerprint is blurry or smudged, many examiners have access to computerized enhancement systems that can make prints sharper and clearer. In some labs, examiners have the computer capability to take digital snapshots of a fingerprint on a hard-to-see background (a colorful soda can, for instance) and then manipulate the image to "float" the print off the can. "We cancel out the background," says forensic expert Susan Narveson, "which gives us a lot better chance to capture the detail of the print."[45]

Invisible Fingerprints

Many fingerprints are latent prints, invisible until special chemicals are applied. Experience guides examiners in their choice of which chemical to use. Small Particle Reagent (a suspension of molybdenum disulfide in detergent) works well on nonporous, wet plastic bags, glass, and firearms. Iodine fumes bring up invisible prints left on rubber gloves. Ninhydrin can develop fingerprints on porous items including paper; gentian violet is effective for prints left on sticky adhesives; and diaminobenzidine reacts well with enzymes in blood to produce visible prints after the color is gone. FBI examiner Tim Trozzi points out, "It's a combination of skill, experience, and intuition, . . . and sometimes it's a bit of luck. You have to start by considering the nature of the object you're examining, how long the print might have been there, what type of atmospheric conditions it's been subjected to."[46]

Since the mid-1970s, lasers have been widely used to illuminate invisible prints. After a room is darkened, the laser is passed over the suspect surface and the prints shine out. Lasers are popular because they leave no residue and will not damage the evidence. They are also valuable for use on prints that have been on a surface for a long time. On the downside, they are expensive—one laser used in the FBI crime lab cost $65,000—so smaller crime labs cannot afford them. A portable fingerprinting tool that may be used at crime scenes is a RU-VIS or reflective ultraviolet imaging system. Like a laser, it uses special light that helps illuminate latent prints, as well as other types of evidence.

Finding Latent Fingerprints

Latent fingerprints are not visible to the naked eye. Depending on the object and quality of the prints, forensic technicians use four different methods to locate and preserve latent prints.

Exposing the fingerprints to a special light will sometimes cause the prints to appear.

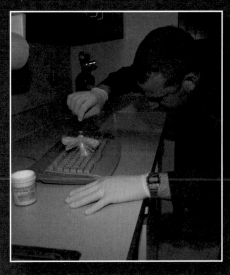

A soft brush is used to dust a fine, colored powder over the surface of the evidence. The powder sticks to the latent prints.

The dusted print is covered with clear, sticky tape and carefully lifted off. The tape is placed on a plastic card for later comparison.

Instead of dusting, steam from an iron is sometimes applied to porous materials like paper and cardboard to bring prints into view.

Super-Glue Fuming

One chemical compound that has gained unexpected popularity in highlighting latent fingerprints is cyanoacrylate, also known as super glue. The super-glue fuming method was discovered almost simultaneously in Britain, Japan, and Canada, when technicians noticed that they could see their fingerprints developing during the process of super-gluing a piece of lab equipment. A little experimentation proved that the glue adheres to amino acids left on a surface, and the visible print created is almost impossible to remove.

When using the super-glue fuming method today, lab technicians place the article that is going to be checked for fingerprints in an airtight tank along with a small heater. A few drops of liquid super glue in a dish are placed inside, the tank is sealed, and the heater turned on. With heat, the super glue turns into a gas, and in a few minutes any prints become visible and impervious to smudging. The technique produces outstanding results on all nonporous surfaces like metal, glass, and plastic, and has been known to work on porous surfaces, too, even human skin. Forensic experts Henry C. Lee and R.E. Gaensslen provide a cautionary note about the latter, however: "Generally, hairless areas of smooth skin on a fresh body are more likely to yield identifiable latent prints . . . [but] success rates are very low."[47]

Lips, Ears, and Palms

Although fingerprints remain the standard for identifying individuals, many law enforcement agencies regularly take palm prints of suspects as well. Palm print databases are being created in several large cities. Some experts have also turned to lip and ear prints in attempts to identify perpetrators.

No definitive study has been done in the United States to prove that ear and lip prints are as unique as fingerprints. Japanese scientists, however, have conducted extensive research on lip imprints for criminal identification, and British scientists have developed a computerized system that allows them to identify ear prints easily as well. Professor Guy Rutty, head of the forensic pathology unit at the University of Leeds in England, states, "Basically we have brought it up to speed and modernised things considerably. We've produced a computerised system for identifying ear prints along the lines of the fingerprint system."[48]

Palm Prints on Trial

The first use of a palm print as evidence in the identification and conviction of a murderer occurred in a Nevada case involving a stagecoach driver named Fred Searcy, found shot to death on December 5, 1916. Searcy's mail sacks had been slashed open and $4,000 in gold was missing.

A local miner, Ben Kuhl, was charged with the crime and brought to trial. The evidence against Kuhl was largely circumstantial, but included a letter from Searcy's mail pouch smeared with a bloody palm print. Two experts from California police departments testified that the print was made by Kuhl. The defense argued that palm prints were "like handwriting, just a matter of opinion" and could not conclusively be identified as

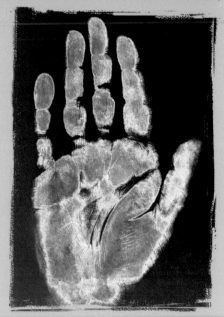

Experts have found that palm prints are as distinctive as fingerprints.

Kuhl's. To prove otherwise, one of the experts persuaded the judge to allow him to examine several palm prints taken from persons in the courtroom, all of which he correctly matched to their owners. On October 6, 1917, the jury returned a guilty verdict; Kuhl's conviction was upheld on appeal by the Nevada Supreme Court.

In at least one case in the United States—the murder of James McCann, who was beaten to death in his home in 1997—investigators identified a perpetrator through the partial print of one of his ears. David Wayne Kunze was convicted of the murder in part because his ear print was found on the wall outside the bedroom where McCann was killed. Experts made the match after Kunze agreed to provide a print by putting hand lotion on his ear and pressing it against a glass surface. The print was then dusted and transferred onto a transparent plastic overlay.

Despite the match, Kunze's conviction was overturned after an appeals court disallowed the ear print evidence. They claimed that the identification method did not meet scientific standards. Despite the negative judgment, impression specialists believe that ear prints will eventually be accepted in U.S. courts, just as they are in other countries. Author Katherine Ramsland writes, "It's a matter of proving the theory that nature doesn't repeat itself, and earprints, like fingerprints, show a unique design."[49]

Shoes and Tires

Shoe prints left at a crime scene can be almost as valuable as fingerprints. In at least one case, a bruise impression in the shape of a shoe found on a murdered child's body led directly to a killer. Bill Bodziak, a world renowned FBI expert on footwear evidence, explains:

> I could determine the size and the design of the shoe. . . . I was able to determine that the contusions [bruises] had been made by a deck shoe whose heel was worn down, and I could see precisely where the stitching had gone into the heel. Stitching is done randomly; no two shoes are alike. Using the stitching holes, I was able to match the impression on that little girl's skin to the suspect's shoe. It was the footwear impression that . . . got us the conviction.[50]

Shoe prints may not be the exact size of the suspect's shoe due to slippage or other distortion, but identifying marks on the soles, such as unusual wear patterns, marks of repair, pebbles caught in the tread, or random damage caused by normal use can make a print one-of-a-kind. These are known as individual characteristics and can match the print with a particular shoe to the exclusion of all other shoes. If not enough detail is present, the print still may provide enough information to identify the shoe's make, model, and size. In the case of athletic footwear, the detailed patterns on the soles make them relatively easy to

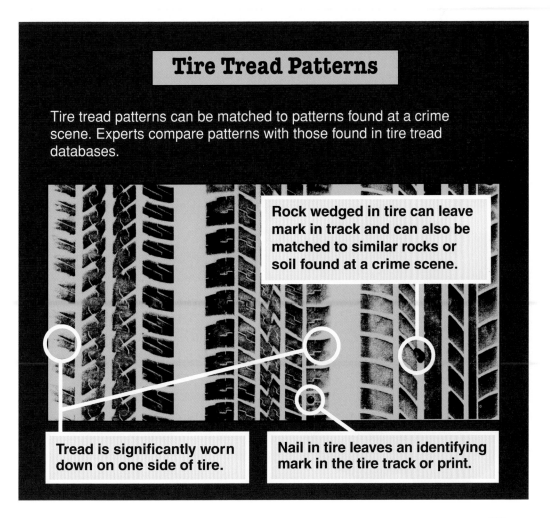

Tire Tread Patterns

Tire tread patterns can be matched to patterns found at a crime scene. Experts compare patterns with those found in tire tread databases.

Rock wedged in tire can leave mark in track and can also be matched to similar rocks or soil found at a crime scene.

Tread is significantly worn down on one side of tire.

Nail in tire leaves an identifying mark in the tire track or print.

identify, especially because athletic footwear manufacturers keep records of the patterns and designs they use for their shoes.

Impressions of tires can be as distinctive as those of athletic shoes. Some tread patterns are S shaped, some run in the shape of a V, and some have crosshatches on the left and parallel lines on the right. There are also other characteristics that distinguish one tire from another. For instance, some tires are bald or have little tread. Some are narrower than others. Some are worn more on one side than the other.

In the case of Florida murderer Bobby Jo Long, his tires had distinctively different tread patterns, and this detail caught investigators' attention. The mismatched prints, found near the body of Michelle Denise Simms, were sent to a tire expert, who went through tire catalogs and identified them as having been made by a Goodyear Viva tire and a Vogue Tyre, the latter an expensive brand that was relatively rare. From the size of these tires, the expert could also deduce that the suspect was driving a medium or full-sized car. That information matched the Dodge Magnum with mismatched tires that Bobby Jo Long owned, and helped to convict him after he was apprehended in 1984.

A bite from an apple can leave an identifiable impression.

"Where Bite Marks Are Present"

In the absence of fingerprints, shoe prints, or tire impressions, bite marks can sometimes be used to bring the guilty to justice. A hungry killer might grab a bite of apple from a victim's refrigerator or spit out chewing gum into a wastepaper basket. Cheese and chocolate have been found to retain teeth impressions, too. The most common place where investigators find bite marks, however, is on the human body, particularly the body of a female victim who has been sexually assaulted and killed. Such impressions can be difficult for a nonexpert to identify with certainty, so any rough-

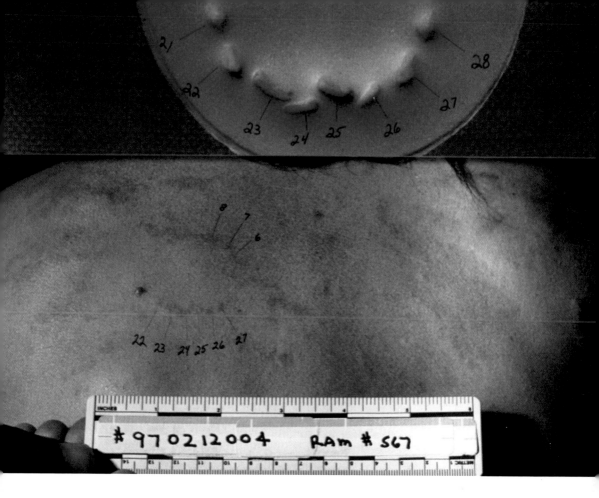

ly semicircular bruise about two inches in diameter on the body is commonly treated as suspicious, and a forensic odontologist is called in to examine it.

To determine whether the bruise one is looking at is a bite or not, an odontologist uses special lights to bring up details that are invisible under normal white light. Forensic expert Anil Aggrawal notes: "Human saliva shines brightly in UV light. Wherever the attacker has bitten his victim, his saliva stains are bound to be there, although they may dry. . . . These saliva stains start shining and we can immediately know that this is the place where bite marks are present."[51]

Once positively identified, a bite mark can reveal a unique pattern of cuts and bruises that cannot be easily reproduced by someone else's teeth. This is because everyone's bite is different—teeth are crooked, spaced, bucked, broken, or missing in a wide variety of ways. A murderer with prominent canine

Bite marks (bottom) are measured and compared with an impression of the alleged biter's teeth (top) to determine if there is a match.

molars, for instance, will leave exceptionally large, dark bruises where those teeth have pressed on the skin. A person with buck teeth will leave a sharp-arched bruise pattern, while someone with crooked teeth will leave bruises that are crooked. An odontologist armed with a mold of the suspect's upper and lower bite can usually prove a match simply by fitting the molds to the bruises on the skin.

Odontologists often go one step further, however, and examine the bite mark under the electron microscope as well. This allows them to see the tiniest of impressions or tears in the skin and match them to a suspect set of teeth. If the bite mark is faint, image-enhancing software can be used to make its features more visible as well.

A bite mark on human skin is a strong indication of guilt, because bites are not linked with ordinary daily activities. Forensic odontologist Michael West explains: "You have to be in a violent contact with that individual to deposit a bite mark. In that light, bite marks are better than fingerprints, because they not only show that you were present, they show you were in a violent confrontation with that individual."[52]

One of the first bite-mark cases to be tried in the United States occurred in the 1970s, when serial killer Ted Bundy was on trial for murdering several college students on the campus of Florida State University in Tallahassee. In addition to being a brutal, sadistic killer, Bundy enjoyed biting his victims both during and after his sexual assaults. When clear bite-mark wounds on the body of one of his victims, twenty-year-old Lisa Levy, were compared with an impression of Bundy's teeth, they were shown to be a perfect match. As a result, Bundy was found guilty and was executed for his crimes in 1989.

By the Numbers

72

Number of murders Ted Bundy was suspected of but never charged with

Despite the growing use of bite-mark evidence, some experts warn that care must be taken when such impressions are analyzed. Different people can leave similar bite impressions, and when bites are made, the skin can shift, leaving an inaccurate mark. "They have their place," says Edward Woolridge, a forensic odontologist from North Carolina. "But I know there's innocent people in jail because of bite-mark testimony."[53]

Tool Marks

Tool marks are not as strong a link between victim and killer as bite marks are, but experts often use them to prove how a crime was committed and whether a certain tool is a murder weapon or not. Tools that leave impressions include screwdrivers, scissors, knives, pliers, wrenches, crowbars, hammers, saws, wire, and chains. The type of mark these tools leave falls into two categories: compression marks and scraping or striated marks.

A forensic odontologist testifies in the 1979 trial that only Ted Bundy's teeth could have made the bite marks found on one of his victims.

Using a laser, a forensic specialist tests a gun for fingerprints.

Compression marks are those left when a tool is pushed or forced into a material that can pick up its impression. This might be the circular mark of a hammer on a victim's skull or the linear shape of a screwdriver blade left on a wooden windowsill that was pried open. Scraping or striated marks are produced by a combination of pressure and sliding. An example might be marks left by a bolt cutter on a chain or a saw cutting through bone.

To make matches, experts in the lab must have both the tool and the object on which its impression was made. They usually make their comparative examination by preparing test marks using the tool, then comparing those marks to the evidence tool marks. The comparison is often aided by preparing silicone rubber casts of the impressed marks. The casts are easily viewed under the comparison microscope.

The Helle Craft murder case forced forensic experts to make one of the most unusual matches between a body and a tool, which in this case was a wood chipper, a large machine used for cutting wood into tiny pieces. When Craft disappeared in 1986 and her husband was seen running the large power-driven machine in a snowstorm in the middle of the night, crime investigators postulated that he had killed her and run her body through the chipper. A search was instituted, and eventually tiny fragments of human bone were recovered from the scene. These were closely examined. At trial, a wood expert was able to testify that, based on the striations found on the bone fragments, the chipper model used by Richard Craft had produced them. In 1989 Craft was found guilty and sentenced to ninety-nine years in prison.

Bullets and Firearms

Unlike Richard Craft, who investigators believe beat his wife to death before disposing of her body, many killers shoot their victims. When bullets and cartridge cases are collected at the crime scene and taken to the lab, investigators know that they have to look for a special type of impression evidence—that created by the gun itself.

When a gun is fired, the firing pin slams into the base of a cartridge, leaving a small indentation known as a firing pin impression. Any imperfections such as nicks or scratches in the firing pin are transferred into the firing pin impression on the cartridge. These and other marks can be used to identify the gun that fired a particular bullet. Rifling marks—spiral ridges and grooves—are also impressed on the bullet as it passes along the barrel of a gun that has been rifled (designed to increase its accuracy). Because microscopic defects in each gun barrel are unique, the patterns carved on a particular bullet are different from those made by any other gun.

Under a comparison microscope, forensic experts line up the markings of two bullets.

A forensic expert restores a gun's serial number with an acidic solution. Suspects sometimes try to avoid detection by filing off the serial number.

Before any analysis can take place, a suspect gun of the right caliber and type must be located for comparison. Then, because firearm experts cannot directly compare marks on a bullet or cartridge case to the barrel or firing pin of a gun, they must test-fire the suspect weapon, usually into a large volume of water that slows the bullet's flight without damaging it. This generates a sample from the gun that will be used for microscopic examination and comparison.

The two bullets to be compared are mounted side by side, and one is rotated to locate a prominent group of striations. The other bullet is then rotated in an attempt to find identical striations. The study of the surface of the two samples continues until the examiner can say for certain whether they were or were not fired through the same barrel.

Many laboratories today employ image databases of fired cartridge cases. Authors Joe Nickell and John F. Fischer explain further: "Markings on a bullet or shell are typically recorded by microscope and video camera and then are digitally translated for computer storage. The computer can subsequently report those files with similar characteristics so that an examiner can then manually compare them and perhaps make a match."[54]

"Happy Birthday, Friend!"

Just as fingers, teeth, tools, and guns leave their own kind of impression evidence, so, too, do pens and pencils. Experts have found that writing or printing not only makes an impression on the fibers of the paper being written on but leaves indentations on the pages beneath it. This is known as indented writing, and it is another form of evidence that can be used to catch a killer.

Investigators look for indented writing any time they see a tablet or some other writing surface at a crime scene. They have discovered that people may throw away incriminating notes but often forget that their pen or pencil might have made an impression on whatever lies beneath. Such was the case in 1986 when a Massachusetts man was found murdered on his birthday. A note found next to his body read, "Happy Birthday, Friend!"

Crime investigators soon learned that the victim was the boyfriend of a woman whose ex-lover was very jealous. During a search of the ex-lover's car, they found an envelope with the woman's name and address on it. When it was submitted to the documents lab for comparison of the handwriting, the examiner, Jim Gerhardt, made a stunning discovery: "I was working in an office with a window looking east. . . . As the sun rose behind me, sunlight streamed into my office at a very low angle. I just

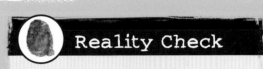

Reality Check

Can a gun be traced if its serial number is filed off?

The serial-number stamping process affects the metal beneath the surface numbers. Examiners can restore the numbers by first grinding the metal to remove any file marks. They then apply a solution of copper salts and hydrochloric acid to the smooth surface. The metal directly beneath the stamped numbers dissolves at a faster rate than the metal around them, which temporarily causes the numbers to reappear long enough for examiners to photograph them.

happened to glance at the envelope—and I saw that there was indented writing on it. When I looked at it more closely, I could see that the indentions read, 'Happy Birthday, Friend!'"[55] It was later proven that the ex-lover had been sitting in his car when he wrote the note, using the envelope as backing. He had then gone inside, killed his victim, and left the note.

Gerhardt relied on oblique lighting to view the above sample of indented writing. Many experts, though, turn to electrostatic detection apparatus (ESDA) when they attempt to view such impression evidence in the lab. ESDA utilizes a process in which electrostatic material (usually black copy machine toner) is sprinkled over the suspect page. An electric charge in the machine then causes the toner to migrate to depressions in the paper, filling in the indented writing.

Distinctive print impressions made by dust on a photocopier help a San Diego Police Department document examiner analyze the source of the copies.

Using ESDA, indented writing may be recovered three, four, or even more pages below the original page of writing. This was highlighted in one Oregon case in which a female felon convicted of murder escaped from prison. Detectives who found a tablet in her cell used ESDA to discover a rough map and street address on the fourth page. The woman was tracked down and arrested within days of her escape.

Identified or Excluded?

Not every piece of evidence can be as dramatic or as conclusive as the incident of the tablet in the cell. Examiners often work long and hard before they identify or exclude a sample of evidence they are considering. An identification means that a clear, definitive match has been made between two things such as a fingerprint and a suspect. An exclusion means there is definitely no match between the items that are being compared. Just one point of difference in a comparison study disqualifies an item for a match. In a depressing number of cases, examiners discover that evidence is too scant, blurred, or marred in some way for any kind of determination to be made. Then they must state that their examination is "inconclusive" and put the evidence aside as useless, at least for the time being.

Document examiners compare the known handwriting of a person (bottom) to see if it matches a sample believed to be from him or her (top).

Even when the most skilled analysts view the evidence, disagreements often arise over their determinations. Such disagreements are highlighted in the courtroom, where both defense and prosecution lawyers rely on expert testimony to make their case but challenge even the clearest evidence the other side presents. When that happens, most experts, like Neil Kaye, a forensic psychiatrist from Delaware who has testified in several high-profile cases, try to remain philosophical about the challenges. "If everybody agreed, there wouldn't need to be a trial," Kaye notes. "Two very bright people can evaluate the same information and come to different conclusions. It happens in everyday life, and it happens in other scientific fields."[56]

CHAPTER 5

"The Bad Guy Is . . . Yours"

By the time they have completed their analysis of all the evidence found at the crime scene, forensic experts have generally established a scenario of what took place during the murder they are helping investigate. They may have learned who the victim was and where and how he or she was killed. They probably have formed a rough estimate of when the murder took place. Sometimes, but not always, they have helped identify a perpetrator or narrowed down the possibilities to a suspect or two as well.

If the alleged perpetrator has been identified and arrested, the experts testify to what they know at the murder trial. There, they can find their conclusions disputed by other experts who interpret the scientific facts in a different way. They can also face allegations of improper investigatory procedures, accusations of a broken chain of custody, and challenges to techniques that some in the scientific or legal community consider unproven. Ramsland notes that DNA procedures once fell in this questionable category:

> [In 1987] DNA testing had not yet been accepted into court and before it could be used, it had to go through a pretrial hearing. Any time new scientific technology is introduced as testimony, it must pass certain tests of acceptability in the scientific community. That way the courts can avoid admitting evidence based on whim or junk science. DNA analysis had to prove to be scientifically sound in method, theory, and interpretation, and positively reviewed by peers.[57]

Kathleen Hunt Atwater Peterson- Injuries

Elizabeth Ann McKee Ratliff- Injuries

Analysis carried out by forensic experts is presented to jurors during a murder trial.

Crime Scene Reconstruction

Even after experts have already satisfied themselves as to the facts gathered regarding a case, they must review those facts and reconstruct events with lawyers who are getting ready to try the case. If a long period of time has passed, they are no longer able to return to the crime scene and thus must rely on notes, photos, and saved exhibits such as bone fragments or bloodstained clothing when doing their review. Forensic technician Daryl Clemens notes, "The reconstructionist should examine all scene photographs, autopsy protocol and photographs, measurements, drawings, notes, reports and items of evidence."[58]

Reconstructing a crime from forensic evidence can sometimes be difficult if there is little hard evidence on which to base deductions. In the 2002 Laci and Conner Peterson double murder, for instance, no blood or signs of violence defined the crime scene in Modesto, California. No murder weapon was found. When Laci's body washed ashore in San Francisco Bay, it was too decomposed to yield such vitals as means or time of death.

Onlookers view a replica of Scott Peterson's boat. Forensic experts found incriminating evidence in the actual boat.

Forensic evidence was limited to a single strand of her hair found in Scott Peterson's recently purchased boat, a boat she had never set foot in.

Prosecutors had to focus on Scott's history of deception, his suspicious behavior around the time of the murder, and the locale where the bodies washed ashore (near where he claimed to have been fishing on the day of Laci's disappearance) to make their case. "This is a circumstantial case, but each piece fits,"[59] prosecutor Rick Distaso told the jury during closing arguments. They agreed and found Laci's husband, Scott, guilty of both murders in November 2004.

Though a lack of forensic evidence characterized the Peterson trial, in other murder cases, forensic experts are able to reconstruct a clearer picture of what happened. Such was the case with the murder of Donna Lynn Vetter in San Antonio, Texas, in 1986. Vetter was a twenty-two-year-old FBI employee who was raped and murdered in her apartment. When a crime team examined the scene, they noted that a screen had been pulled out of the front window and a plant had been knocked over inside that window. The phone had also been unplugged. The victim had been struck in the face, stabbed repeatedly with one of her own kitchen knives, and then sexually assaulted. The knife was found hidden under a cushion in the living room.

From this information, the crime team deduced that the perpetrator had entered the house through the front window with sexual assault, not murder, on his mind. He had taken nothing from the house. He had disconnected the telephone in order to keep Vetter from using it, something he would not have done if he had planned to kill her. When the need to kill arrived, he had used a weapon of opportunity—one of her knives—rather than one of his own.

By the Numbers

30

Percentage of female murder victims in the United States who are killed by their husbands or boyfriends

With the help of a blood spatter expert who looked at the height and direction of bloodstains in the Vetter house, investigators were able to determine that the victim had first been struck while standing in the bathroom. Blood spatter in the kitchen indicated that the attack continued there, and a blood trail could be followed through the dining room to the living room, where Vetter's body was found.

"Into the Mind of the Criminal"

Reconstruction provides answers about what happened and how it happened, but when there are no likely suspects to consider in a crime, investigators often turn to forensic profilers. Profilers are usually psychologists who specialize in behavior, emotions, and motives. They study the crime scene to determine such things as the killer's age, race, educational background, and lifestyle, all of which can be valuable in the search. Jon Zonderman writes, "The behaviorists seek to get into the mind of the criminal and explore his (or her) thought processes in an attempt to tell investigators what kind of person would commit such a crime and narrow the field of potential suspects by describing . . . characteristics of the person."[60]

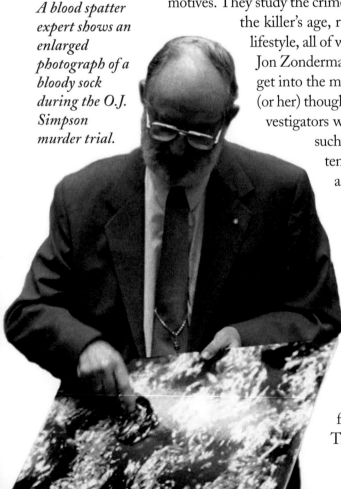

A blood spatter expert shows an enlarged photograph of a bloody sock during the O.J. Simpson murder trial.

One of the first characteristics profilers like to determine is whether the killer has an organized or disorganized personality. Disorganized killers are those who have done little planning for the murder, take enormous risks, and often make little effort to hide their victims. They are commonly below average in intelligence or suffer from mental illness. Richard Trenton Chase, the "vampire of

The Double-Breasted Suit

One of the first cases of criminal profiling took place in New York City in the 1950s. For sixteen years a bomber had been planting explosives in public places such as Radio City Music Hall and Grand Central Station, as well as sending angry letters to local newspapers, politicians, and utility companies. Unable to identify a suspect, New York City police tried an unconventional approach. They turned for help to criminal psychiatrist James Brussel.

Brussel studied the case and then provided the police with predictions of the bomber's ethnicity, approximate age, living situation, and even preferred clothing. According to Brussel's profile, the perpetrator was a male mechanic. He was extremely neat and tidy and dressed in double-breasted suits. He had once worked for Con Edison, the electric utility to which the bomber had sent letters. He was most likely middle aged and lived with a maiden sister or aunt in Connecticut.

Psychiatrist Dr. James Brussel developed an amazingly accurate profile of a serial bomber.

With the help of Con Edison records, the police finally identified a suspect in 1957: George Metesky of Waterbury, Connecticut. As Brussel had predicted, Metesky lived with two unmarried sisters and matched the profile in age, ethnicity, and religion. He had also been injured while working at Con Edison. When the police arrived at his door, Metesky met them in his robe and politely confessed to being the bomber. Instructed to get dressed, he went to his room and returned wearing a double-breasted suit.

Sacramento," who believed he needed to drink his victims' blood in order to survive, epitomized this type of killer. Organized killers, on the other hand, are highly intelligent and more methodical in their killing. FBI profiler Russell Vorpagel writes, "The [organized] offender takes precautions against discovery of himself. Few, if any weapons or fingerprints are found. The crime appears to be deliberate, calculated, and pre-planned. Investigators find little evidence to work with in developing a profile."[61] Ted Bundy and John Wayne Gacy were two examples of organized killers.

Profilers look at other aspects of the crime scene to help understand the killer, too. They even study the victim's lifestyle, personality, occupation, and activities, since these may have brought him or her to the killer's notice. They evaluate every detail of the killing itself. If an offender broke into a house through a locked window, for instance, the profiler knows that the offender is likely a criminal burglar. If the killer remained in the home for a time after the murder, they know the person was relatively comfortable in the surroundings and perhaps had been there before. He or she may have been a friend of the victim.

Profiling can be a powerful tool in narrowing the field to a certain type of suspect, but even profilers agree that it does not substitute for a thorough murder investigation or hard evidence such as fingerprints or DNA. No person is ever tried and convicted solely on the basis of profiling. Some critics even judge the field of profiling to be "junk" (unproven) science. Vorpagel notes, "Our work was viewed, back in the seventies, as being close to soothsaying [witchcraft]. . . . The basic psychology is still not accepted by a lot of educated people."[62]

Expert Witness

Though profilers can help bring about the arrest of a killer, they seldom serve as expert witnesses in a murder trial. Instead, a wide variety of other types of crime experts are called on to explain certain aspects of forensic evidence. Whether they represent the defense or the prosecution, they are responsible for

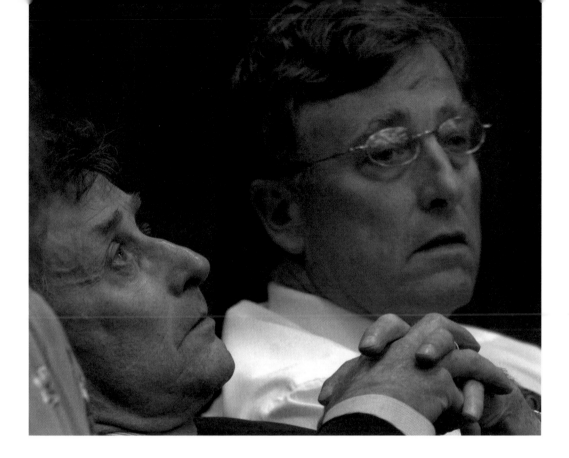

presenting the facts as clearly and accurately as possible. They must also know the case thoroughly so they can have the necessary facts at their fingertips and testify with confidence. Michael Baden writes, "When it comes to testifying, it is important for an expert witness to review in detail all of his findings and opinions with the attorney. This is called preparation. . . . In my opinion, the three most important factors in testimony are preparation, preparation and preparation."[63]

Well-prepared and well-qualified forensic experts are invaluable in court because they provide a wealth of information about a little-known topic. Baden and Roach note, "The jury needs to know that the expert witness is in the courtroom to provide specialized information to assist it in interpreting the factual evidence."[64] At times, the assistance can be unique and enthralling, as when, in the trial of Michael Peterson for the 2001 death of his wife Kathleen, in Durham, North Carolina, Henry Lee demonstrated blood spatter by spitting ketchup on poster board in the courtroom.

Accused murderer Michael Peterson (left) awaits a verdict in his murder trial in 2003.

Pollen Forensics

In the future, courts will have to judge the validity of new kinds of forensic sciences. A little known field called forensic palynology—the use of pollen and spores to solve crime—could be one of them, as an article entitled "Pollen Forensics May Help in Fight Against Terrorism," published at Texas A&M University in April 2003 explains:

Forensic palynology . . . begins with determining the "pollen print" of a geographical region, Texas A&M University anthropologist Vaughn Bryant says. Much like a fingerprint identifies a person, a "pollen print" identifies a specific geographical region, he explains. It consists of the microscopic pollen grains and spores from plants inhabiting a certain area, which are in a ratio to one another unique to that area, he says.

Knowing the pollen print of a particular crime scene can enable investigators to compare pollen samples from a suspect's clothing, shoes or even vehicle and determine if a match exists with the scene. . . . While not always producing a definitive result, there are instances . . . when the evidence is so substantial it can build a compelling case against a suspect.

For example, in New Zealand—a country leading the world in the use of forensic palynology—criminal investigators were able to link a suspect to a remote area in a park where a woman was raped and murdered. . . . The crime scene had a specific plant cover, mainly fern and pine, that only occurred in that area of the park. The suspect, who had denied ever visiting that area of the park, was linked to the scene after clothes from his hamper were impounded by police and analyzed for pollen content. Not only did his clothes match the pollen print of the crime scene, . . . but the only way he could have accumulated the amount of pollen present on his clothes was to literally roll around in that area of the park.

Sometimes it can be controversial. This is because, although forensic evidence is grounded in scientific fact, it can be complex and has to be interpreted. Even the best experts do not always agree in their interpretations. Such was the case in the murder trial of Sandra Murphy and Richard Tabish, a couple accused of killing millionaire playboy Ted Binion in 1998. At their trial in 2000, Cyril Wecht, a renowned forensic pathologist, was a witness for the defense and testified that Binion died of an overdose of drugs—heroin and tranquilizers. Michael Baden, famed in his own right, served as an expert for the prosecution. He noticed minute hemorrhages in Binion's eyes and testified that the millionaire had been "burked," a form of asphyxiation that leaves few traces. The jury agreed with the prosecution and found the couple guilty. (After the Supreme Court overturned the conviction in 2003, a second trial took place in 2004. This time, faced with the same forensic evidence, the jury

A police officer points to the bloody glove found near the body of Nicole Brown Simpson. Problems with evidence collection surfaced during the trial of her ex-husband, O.J. Simpson.

sided with the defense's testimony and found Murphy and Tabish innocent.)

In some instances, expert witnesses are ultimately not as helpful as they should be. Some are boring or confusing. Others are sloppy, and when evidence they handled proves to have been carelessly collected and stored, or if the chain of custody was broken, the opposition can effectively claim that they are basing their opinions on faulty evidence. The O.J. Simpson case was an example of faulty evidence collection and protection; vials of blood were left unprotected in a hot van and a back gate was not photographed, so blood smears later found there were questionable.

Age of Homicide Victims and Offenders in the United States

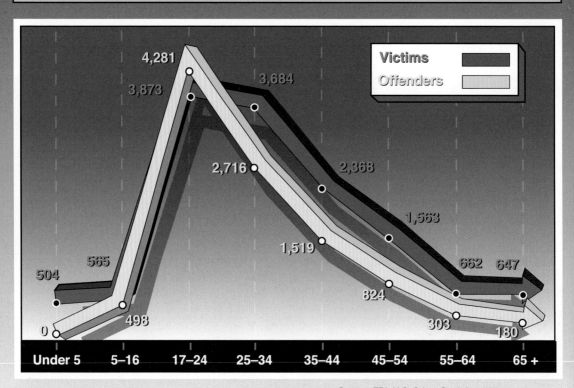

Source: FBI, U.S. Crime Statistics, 2004.

While shortcomings in the Simpson case may have been due to simple mistakes, in other instances, crime investigators who serve as expert witnesses have been proven to be biased and even corrupt. Two such men were West Virginia forensics expert Fred Zain and Texas pathologist Ralph Erdmann. Both repeatedly falsified evidence and committed perjury in court in order to support law enforcement's theories of a suspect's guilt and maintain their privileged positions. They were undoubtedly not the only two to yield to such temptation, as Lee observes: "Any procedure in scientific testing is only as good as the scientist's ability to perform such a test. . . . It is not unprecedented to learn that incorrect or fraudulent results were reported by forensic pathologists and forensic scientists."[65]

Relationship of U.S. Murderers to Their Victims

Unknown Relationship 44%

Family 13%

13% Stranger

30% Other Known (friends, coworkers)

Source: FBI, U.S. Crime Statistics, 2004.

Admissibility of Evidence

Because forensic evidence is becoming increasingly important in court, forensic investigators must be careful to collect, protect, and document every piece of evidence at the scene. They must also ensure that evidence is analyzed as carefully and as objectively as possible.

On the other hand, it is the court's responsibility to ensure that evidence based on unproven science is not used at trial. To aid them in their determinations, judges have guidelines regarding what is true science and what is not. Many state courts screen forensic testimony in accordance with the 1923 federal decision *Frye v. United States. Frye* (as it is called) holds that expert testimony must be based on principles "sufficiently established to have gained general acceptance in the particular field in which it belongs."[66] This means that not only are fingerprint experts accepted in court but experts in lip or ear prints—disciplines that are still questionable in the United States—might be allowed as well.

Federal courts and some state courts that work to ensure that only the most valid scientific evidence is admitted follow the stricter 1993 *Daubert* standard, which was named after a Supreme Court decision in the case *Daubert v. Merrell Dow Pharmaceuticals, Inc.* This decision states that federal judges "must ensure that any and all scientific testimony or evidence admitted is not only relevant, but reliable,"[67] meaning that evidence must be based on disciplines that have been tested, studied, and written about in scientific journals, in addition to being well accepted throughout the scientific community. Andre A. Moenssens, an expert in the oft-challenged field of handwriting analysis, says of judges who prefer the *Daubert* stan-

Magnification helps investigators identify the characteristics of a bullet.

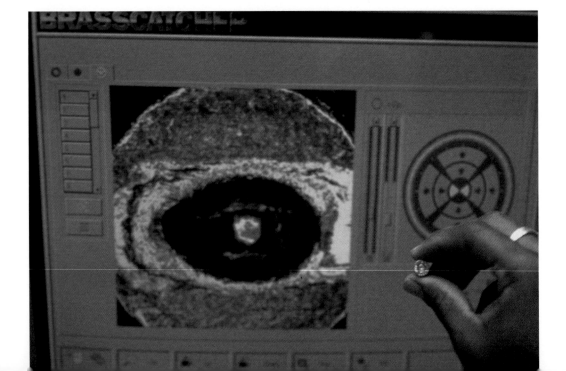

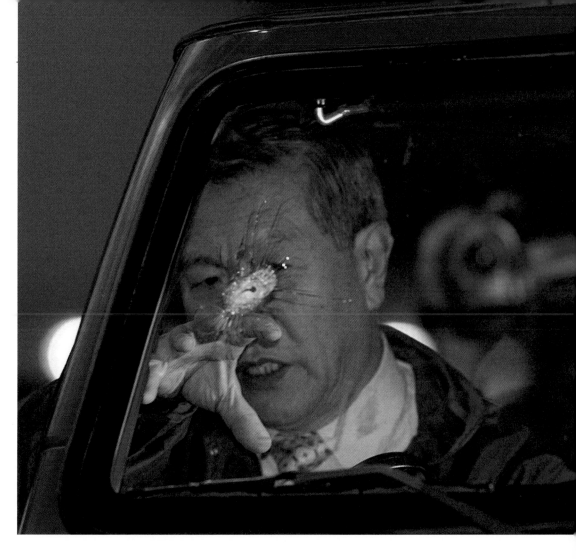

dard: "Expect to be challenged on everything. Today, that also includes things that are outside your own professional competence, but that relate to your field. You should also stay current on the pertinent case law that has been handed down, not only in your own jurisdiction, but also elsewhere."[68]

Even aided by such guidelines, courts are likely to remain busy indefinitely, deciding if new forensic technologies such as brain fingerprinting and computer reenactments of crimes are valid science or not. Brain fingerprinting is a method of reading the brain's involuntary electrical activity in response to seeing certain images relating to a crime. Although the FBI seems to support it, critics believe it needs more study before its use becomes widespread and cases are won or lost on its

Forensic expert Dr. Henry Lee inspects a crime scene. The work of Lee and other forensic scientists has contributed hugely to crime-solving efforts.

evidence. And regarding computer reenactments, Baden and Roach comment:

> Software has the ability to provide a feeling for what probably happened at the crime scene by filling in sketchy evidence to yield an explanation. Is that misleading a jury or leading it effectively to a fair conclusion?. . . If there is a question about the personal ethics or devotion to scientific principles of those inputting the information, the possibility for manipulation is at least equal to that of any other forensic evidence.[69]

While the courts try to decide whether such developments are acceptable or not, there are some types of advances that are widely accepted and will make crime scene analysis easier and more effective. They involve the use of new types of scanners, microscopes, and spectrometers that allow analysts to examine material with greater precision. The process of miniaturizing complex analytical lab equipment—such as portable mass spectrometers—will also improve the way crime scenes are investigated. Such equipment gives investigators the ability to analyze even minute samples in real time, with accuracy equal to or better than that of conventional laboratories. Scientists are already developing a DNA testing chip that would let police analyze blood at the scene immediately, rather than having to ship off samples and wait weeks for results.

Despite such advances, nothing will take the place of the skill, passion, and dedication that talented forensic experts bring to the crime lab. Their work requires endless patience, and their efforts are often overlooked. Nevertheless, the end results are ultimately worthwhile, as journalist Jeffrey Kluger notes: "It's a grueling business of trial and error, of investigative dead ends, of repeating the same experiment over weeks or months, until finally, one day, all the tumblers click into place and the bad guy is at last yours. It isn't prime time [television]—but it's not a bad day's work either."[70]

Notes

Introduction: "Taking in the Evidence, Doing the Work"

1. Quoted in CBSNews.com, "Police: Body Is Lori Hacking," October 1, 2004. www.cbsnews.com/stories/2004 /10/29/national/main652341.shtml.

2. Quoted in Kevin McCullen, "JonBenet Case Follows Investigators," Rocky MountainNews.com, October 25, 1999. http://denver.rockymountainnews.com/ extra/ramsey/1025wick1.shtml.

3. Quoted in Christina S.N. Lewis, "Reviewing 3,000 Cold Cases, One by One," CNN.com, January 31, 2003. www.cnn.com /2003/LAW/01/31/ctv. cold.case.review.

4. Jon Zonderman, *Beyond the Crime Lab: The New Science of Investigation.* New York: John Wiley & Sons, 1999, p. 7.

5. Barry A.J. Fisher, *Techniques of Crime Scene Investigation.* New York: CRC, 2000, p. 20.

6. Quoted in N.E. Genge, *The Forensic Casebook.* New York: Ballantine, 2002, p. 244.

Chapter 1: The Crime Scene

7. Michael Baden and Marion Roach, *Dead Reckoning: The New Science of Catching Killers.* New York: Simon & Schuster, 2001, p. 21.

8. Genge, *The Forensic Casebook*, p. 3.

9. David Fisher, *Hard Evidence.* New York: Simon & Schuster, 1995, p. 21.

10. Fisher, *Techniques of Crime Scene Investigation*, p. 27.

11. Zonderman, *Beyond the Crime Lab*, pp. 83–85.

12. Quoted in Katherine Ramsland, "The Medical Examiner," Crime Library, 2005. www.crimelibrary.com/criminal _mind/ forensics/crimescene/4.html ?sect=21.

13. Baden and Roach, *Dead Reckoning*, p. 145.

14. Tom Harris, "How Luminol Works," How Stuff Works, 2005. http://people. howstuffworks.com/luminol3.htm.

15. Daryl W. Clemens, "An Introduction to Crime Scene Reconstruction for the Criminal Profiler," Crime and Clues, April 1998. www.crimeandclues.com /introduction.htm.

16. Quoted in Katherine Ramsland, "The Forensic Mind—from Evidence to Theory," Crime Library, 2005. www. crimelibrary.com/criminal_mind/ forensics/crimescene/7.html?sect=21.

101

17. Quoted in Fisher, *Hard Evidence*, p. 21.

Chapter 2: Under the Microscope

18. Quoted in *Forensic Nurse*, "Off the Bookshelf," 2005. www.forensicnursemag.com/articles/371newsviews.html.

19. Fisher, *Hard Evidence*, p. 19.

20. Fisher, *Hard Evidence*, p. 12.

21. Fisher, *Hard Evidence*, p. 23.

22. Quoted in Fisher, *Hard Evidence*, pp. 161–62.

23. Katherine Ramsland, "Modern Detection Methods," Crime Library, 2005. www.crimelibrary.com/criminal_mind/forensics/toxicology/10.html?sect=9.

24. Katherine Ramsland, "Hair Evidence Analysis," Crime Library, 2005. www.crimelibrary.com/criminal_mind/forensics/trace/ 5.html?sect=21.

25. Baden and Roach, *Dead Reckoning*, p. 184.

26. Quoted in Genge, *The Forensic Casebook*, p. 82.

27. Quoted in Fisher, *Hard Evidence*, p. 161.

28. Quoted in Fisher, *Hard Evidence*, p. 187.

29. Fisher, *Hard Evidence*, p. 147.

Chapter 3: DNA, Blood, and Bones

30. Genge, *The Forensic Casebook*, p. 142.

31. Quoted in Ramsland, "The Medical Examiner."

32. Baden and Roach, *Dead Reckoning*, p. 31.

33. Katherine Steck-Flynn, "The Role of Entomology in Forensic Investigations," Crime and Clues, 2003. www.crimeandclues.com /entomology_intro.htm.

34. Quoted in Katherine Ramsland, "When the Dead Serve the Living," Crime Library, 2005. www.crimelibrary.com/criminal_mind/forensics/bill_bass/4.html?sect=21.

35. Quoted in Jessica Snyder Sachs, "A Maggot for the Prosecution," *Discover*, November 1998, p. 102.

36. Baden and Roach, *Dead Reckoning*, p. 144.

37. Genge, *The Forensic Casebook*, p. 152.

38. Quoted in Jeffrey Kluger, "How Science Solves Crimes," *Time*, October 21, 2002, p. 36+.

39. Quoted in CNN.com, "DNA Type in Peterson Hearing Becoming Mainstream Justice Tool," November 3, 2003. www.cnn.com/2003/LAW/11/03/laci.peterson.dna.ap.

40. Quoted in DallasNews.com, "Spread of Innocence Projects Seen as 'New Civil Rights Movement,'" June 6, 2002. www.truthinjustice.org/ipspread.htm.

41. Quoted in DallasNews.com, "Spread of Innocence Projects Seen as 'New Civil Rights Movement.'"

42. Quoted in Katherine Ramsland, "Identification," Crime Library, 2005. www.crimelibrary.com/criminal_mind/forensics/anthropology/2.html?sect=21.

43. Genge, *The Forensic Casebook*, p. 21.

Chapter 4: Impressions of a Killer

44. Mike Byrd, "Other Impression Evidence," Crime-Scene-Investigator. net, 2000. www.crime-scene-investigator.net /otherimpressionevidence.html.

45. Quoted in Kluger, "How Science Solves Crimes."

46. Quoted in Fisher, *Hard Evidence*, p. 135.

47. Henry C. Lee and R.E. Gaensslen, *Advances in Fingerprint Technology.* New York: CRC, 2001, p. 150.

48. Quoted in Patricia Reaney, "Scientists Get a Computerised Grip on Ear Prints," [Pakistan] *Daily Times*, March 15, 2004. www.dailytimes.com.pk/ default.asp?page=story_15-3-2004 _pg6_13.

49. Katherine Ramsland, "Earprints," Crime Library, 2005. www. crimelibrary.com/ criminal_mind/forensics/fingerprints /7.html?sect=21.

50. Quoted in Fisher, *Hard Evidence*, p. 221.

51. Anil Aggrawal, "Science in Crime Detection—5: What Do the Bite Marks Tell Us?" July 1993. www.fortunecity. com/ tatooine/williamson/235/sicd005.html.

52. Quoted in Steven Kroft, "Forensic Evidence; Skepticism Surrounding Dr. Michael West's Use of Bite Mark Analysis in Murder Cases," *60 Minutes*, February 17, 2003. www.law-forensic.com/cfr_west _14.htm.

53. Quoted in Flynn McRoberts and Steve Mills, "From the Start, a Faulty Science," *Chicago Tribune*, October 19, 2004, p. 1.

54. Joe Nickell and John F. Fischer, *Crime Science: Methods of Forensic Detection.* Lexington: University of Kentucky Press, 1999, p. 95.

55. Quoted in Fisher, *Hard Evidence*, p. 205.

56. Quoted in Lisa Teachey, "Yates' Fate Hinges on Which Psychiatrist Can Sway Jury," HoustonChronicle.com, March 5, 2002. www.chron.com/cs/ CDA/ssistory.mpl/special/drownings /1279886.

Chapter 5: "The Bad Guy Is . . . Yours"

57. Katherine Ramsland, "DNA in Court," Crime Library, 2005. www. crimelibrary. com/criminal_mind/forensics/dna/6.html ?sect=21.

58. Clemens, "An Introduction to Crime Scene Reconstruction for the Criminal Profiler."

59. Quoted in Louis Sahagun, "Prosecution Rests in Laci Peterson Case," *Boston Globe*, November 2, 2004. www.boston. com/news/ nation/articles/2004/11/02/ prosecution_rests_in_laci_peterson_case.

60. Zonderman, *Beyond the Crime Lab*, p. 130.

61. Russell Vorpagel, *Profiles in Murder: An FBI Legend Dissects Killers and Their Crimes.* New York: Plenum Trade, 1998, p. 33.

62. Vorpagel, *Profiles in Murder*, p. 25.

63. Baden and Roach, *Dead Reckoning*, p. 79.

64. Baden and Roach, *Dead Reckoning*, p. 82.

65. Henry C. Lee, *Cracking Cases: The Science of Solving Crimes*. Amherst, NY: Prometheus, 2002, p. 222.

66. *Frye v. United States*, 1923, Harvard Law School. www.law.harvard.edu/publications/evidenceiii/cases/frye.htm.

67. *Daubert v. Merrell Dow Pharmaceuticals, Inc.*, 1993, FindLaw for Legal Professionals. http://caselaw.lp.findlaw. com/scripts/getcase.pl?court=US&vol=509&i nvol=579.

68. Andre A. Moenssens, "Preparing for a *Daubert* Hearing," Forensic-Evidence. com, June 18, 1999. www.forensic-evi dence. com/site/ID/ID_FBI.html.

69. Baden and Roach, *Dead Reckoning*, p. 246.

70. Kluger, "How Science Solves Crime."

For Further Reading

Books

N.E. Genge, *The Forensic Casebook*. New York: Ballantine, 2002. A relatively lively look at forensics. Includes chapters on evidence, the corpse, and specialties such as odontology and photography.

Henry C. Lee, *Cracking Cases: The Science of Solving Crimes*. Amherst, NY: Prometheus, 2002. Takes the reader through the entire investigative process of five murder cases with world-famous Henry C. Lee, considered by some to be the greatest criminologist in the world.

Joe Nickell and John F. Fischer, *Crime Science: Methods of Forensic Detection*. Lexington: University of Kentucky Press, 1999. The authors explain the science behind criminal investigations into the Lindbergh kidnapping, the O.J. Simpson case, the death of Marilyn Monroe, and others.

David Owen, *Police Lab: How Forensic Science Tracks Down and Convicts Killers*. Buffalo, NY: Firefly, 2002. Discusses current methods of forensic investigation, highlighted by actual cases.

Katherine Ramsland, *The Forensic Science of CSI*. New York: Berkeley, 2001. Explores the forensic science used in the television series *CSI: Crime Scene Investigation*.

Pam Walker and Elaine Wood, *Crime Scene Investigations: Real-Life Science Labs for Grades 6–12*. San Francisco: Jossey-Bass, 2002. Provides labs on topics such as document examination, tool mark examination, glass identification, blood drop analysis, and others.

Web Sites

American Society of Crime Laboratory Directors (www.ascld.org/aboutascld. html). Includes information about the society in addition to educational links, forensic links, merchandise, and other information.

Court TV's Crime Library (www.crime library.com). A collection of more than six hundred nonfiction feature stories on major crimes, criminals, trials, forensics, and criminal profiling by prominent writers.

FBI Crime Laboratory (www.fbi.gov/hq/lab /labhome.htm). Includes a history of the crime laboratory as well as procedures for submitting evidence, guidelines for a crime scene search, and descriptions of various types of evidence and what an analysis can reveal.

Periodicals

Jeffrey Kluger, "How Science Solves Crimes," *Time*, October 21, 2002.

Jessica Snyder Sachs, "A Maggot for the Prosecution," *Discover*, November 1998.

Internet Sources

Tom Harris, "How Luminol Works," How Stuff Works, 2005. http://people.how stuffworks.com/luminol3.htm.

Steven Kroft, "Forensic Evidence; Skepticism Surrounding Dr. Michael West's Use of Bite Mark Analysis in Murder Cases," *60 Minutes*, February 17, 2003. www.law-forensic.com/cfr_west_14.htm.

Patrick Lawless, "Forensic Information: How Experts Collect Evidence," PageWise, 2002. http://okok.essortment.com/foren sicevidenc_ rkgc.htm.

Christina S.N. Lewis, "Reviewing 3,000 Cold Cases, One by One," CNN.com, January 31, 2003. www.cnn.com/2003/ LAW/01/ 31/ctv.cold.case.review.

Douglas P. Lyle, *Forensics for Dummies*. Foster City, CA: IDG Books Worldwide, 2004. http://media.wiley.com/product _data/excerpt/04/07645558/ 0764555804.pdf.

Katherine Ramsland, "Famous Early Profile," Crime Library, 2005. www.crimelibrary. com/criminal_mind/profiling/history _method/3.html?sect=20.

Index

Picture Credits

Maury Aaseng, 8, 25, 27
AFP/Getty Images, 16, 55, 62, 90
Associated Press, AP, 13, 18, 31, 34, 55, 56, 58, 77, 79, 87, 93, 95
© Bettmann/CORBIS, 91
CDC/PHIL/CORBIS, 36
© CORBIS, 42, 81
© Custom Medical Stock Photo, 57
Getty Images, 7, 9, 10, 14, 17, 24, 29, 35, 38, 48, 51, 59, 61, 76
Eric and David Hosking/CORBIS, 45
© Mikael Karlsson/Alamy Images, 71
© Ed Kashi/CORBIS, 47
© Simon Kwong/Reuters/CORBIS, 99
© Landov, 30
Steve Liss/ CORBIS SYGMA, 11, 82, 98
© Carols Lopez-Barillas/ CORBIS, 66
Michael Maass, 33, 43, 69, 84, 85
Mediscan/CORBIS, 41
© Charles O'Rear/CORBIS, 80
© Reuters/CORBIS, 22
© Pete Saloutos/ CORBIS, 73
© Shepard Sherbell/CORBIS SABA, 21, 51 (inset), 52
© Kimberly White/Reuters/CORBIS, 88
© Jim Zuckerman, 39

About the Author

Diane Yancey lives in the Pacific Northwest with her husband,
Michael, their dog, Gelato, and their cats, Newton and Lily.
She has written more than twenty-five books for middle-grade
and high school readers, including *Spies*, *Al Capone*, and *Life
on the Pony Express*.